MESSAGE OF THE FATHERS OF THE CHURCH

General Editor, Thomas Halton

Volume 4

MESSAGE OF THE FATHERS OF THE CHURCH

THE CHURCH

by

Thomas Halton

 Michael Glazier
Wilmington, Delaware

ABOUT THE AUTHOR

THOMAS HALTON holds M.A. and Ph.D degrees in Ancient Classics from University College, Dublin and the Catholic University of America, where he is now Professor of Greek and Latin. He is a past President of the North American Patristic Society and has lectured and written widely on patristic subjects in Europe and North America. He is Editorial Director of *The Fathers of the Church* and *Studies in Christian Antiquity*, and serve on the Editorial Boards of *Second Century* and *Catalogus Translationum*. Recently, he co-authored (with Robert D. Sider), "A Decade of Patristic Scholarship 1970-1979," in two special survey issues of *Classical World*, 76 (1982-83).

First published in 1985 by Michael Glazier, Inc., 1723 Delaware Avenue, Wilmington, Delaware 19806.

Distributed outside U. S., Canada, Australia and Philippines by Geoffrey Chapman, a division of Cassel Ltd., 1 Vincent Square, London SW1P ZPN.

Library of Congress Catalog Card Number: 84-72860
International Standard Book Number:
   Message of the Fathers of the Church series:
     (0-89453-312-6, Paper: 0-89435-340-1, Cloth)
   THE CHURCH
     (0-89453-316-9 Paper)
     (0-89435-344-4, Cloth)

Cover design: Lillian Brulc

Printed in the United States of America

TABLE OF CONTENTS

Acknowledgments

Quotations from *Lumen Gentium* are from *Vatican Council II*, ed. Austin Flannery, O.P., Costello Publishing Co., New York, 1981.

Frequent use has been made of the standard English translations of the Fathers in such series as *Ancient Christian Writers, Fathers of the Church, Ante-Nicene Fathers* and *Nicene and Post-Nicene Fathers*, often with adaptations and sometimes with corrections. In all cases the original Greek and Latin texts have been consulted in the best editions available. All the standard dictionaries and lexica have been consulted for articles on the Church and recent patristic scholarship on the Church has been controlled through the standard bibliographies, especially *Bibliographia Patristica*. Those who know the field well will have no difficulty in seeing how little originality can be claimed for this volume, which nonetheless, it is hoped, will have its uses as a *Lumen Gentium* Revisited after twenty years.

Editor's Introduction

The *Message of the Fathers of the Church* is a companion series to The *Old Testament Message* and The *New Testament Message*. It was conceived and planned in the belief that Scripture and Tradition worked hand in hand in the formation of the thought, life and worship of the primitive Church. Such a series, it was felt, would be a most effective way of opening up what has become virtually a closed book to present-day readers, and might serve to stimulate a revival in interest in Patristic studies in step with the recent, gratifying resurgence in Scriptural studies.

The term "Fathers" is usually reserved for Christian writers marked by orthodoxy of doctrine, holiness of life, ecclesiastical approval and antiquity. "Antiquity" is generally understood to include writers down to Gregory the Great (+604) or Isidore of Seville (+636) in the West, and John Damascene (+749) in the East. In the present series, however, greater elasticity has been encouraged, and quotations from writers not noted for orthodoxy will sometimes be included in order to illustrate the evolution of the Message on particular doctrinal matters. Likewise, writers later than the mid-eighth century will sometimes be used to illustrate the continuity of tradition on matters like sacramental theology or liturgical practice.

An earnest attempt was made to select collaborators on a broad inter-disciplinary and inter-confessional basis, the chief consideration being to match scholars who could handle the Fathers in their original languages with subjects in which they had already demonstrated a special interest and competence. About the only editorial directive given to the selected contributors was that the Fathers, for the most part, should be allowed to speak for themselves and that they should speak in readable, reliable modern English.

Volumes on individual themes were considered more suitable than volumes devoted to individual Fathers, each theme, hopefully, contributing an important segment to the total mosaic of the Early Church, one, holy, catholic and apostolic. Each volume has an introductory essay outlining the historical and theological development of the theme, with the body of the work mainly occupied with liberal citations from the Fathers in modern English translation and a minimum of linking commentary. Short lists of Suggested Further Readings are included; but dense, scholarly footnotes were actively discouraged on the pragmatic grounds that such scholarly shorthand has other outlets and tends to lose all but the most relentlessly esoteric reader in a semipopular series.

At the outset of his *Against Heresies* Irenaeus of Lyons warns his readers "not to expect from me any display of rhetoric, which I have never learned, or any excellence of composition, which I have never practised, or any beauty or persuasiveness of style, to which I make no pretensions." Similarly, modest disclaimers can be found in many of the Greek and Latin Fathers and all too often, unfortunately, they have been taken at their word by an uninterested world. In fact, however, they were often highly educated products of the best rhetorical schools of their day in the Roman Empire, and what they have to say is often as much a lesson in literary and cultural, as well as in spiritual, edification.

St. Augustine, in *The City of God* (19.7), has interesting reflections on the need for a common language in an expanding world community; without a common language a man is more at home with his dog than with a foreigner as far as intercommunication goes, even in the Roman Empire, which imposes on the nations it conquers the yoke of both law and language with a resultant abundance of interpreters. It is hoped that in the present world of continuing language barriers the contributors to this series will prove opportune intepreters of the perennial Christian message.

Thomas Halton

Foreword

The present volume in the series, The Message of the Fathers, follows the format by chapter and paragraph of *Lumen Gentium*, the magisterial document devoted to the subject of the Church by the Second Vatican Council in 1964. The choice of this framework seems opportune in that it provided a classic statement of the role and destiny of the Church in the 20th century, a statement at once bold and forward-looking yet deeply rooted in almost every particular in the words of the Fathers of the primitive Church. *Lumen Gentium* did not propose itself as the last word on ecclesiology, and indeed there have been developments in the subject in the intervening twenty years that will be touched on where appropriate in the present work.

The work can best be used as a patristic commentary on *Lumen Gentium* but hopefully it has a unity and continuity of its own, especially as brief excerpts from the Council document are used as pegs on which to hang the patristic excerpts. I owe special thanks to my friend and collaborator in the series, Thomas Carroll, who suggested that I use this format and provided many other illuminating comments in the course of selecting and editing the patristic texts. A special word of thanks is also due to the publisher of the series, Michael Glazier, and his competent staff, all of whom showed courage and enterprise in undertaking and planning the series, and infinite patience during the long process of bringing it to a conclusion.

Abbreviations

AAS	Acta Apostolicae Sedis
ACW	Ancient Christian Writers
ACO	Acta Conciliorum Oecumenicorum, ed. E.Schwartz
ANF	Ante-Nicene Fathers
CCL	Corpus Christianorum, Series latina
CSCO	Corpus Scriptorum Christianorum Orientalium
CSEL	Corpus Scriptorum Ecclesiasticorum Latinorum
FOTC	Fathers of the Church
GCS	Die griechischen christlichen Schriftsteller
NPNF	Nicene and Post-Nicene Fathers
OECT	Oxford Early Christian Texts
PG	Migne, Patrologia Graeca
PL	Migne, Patrologia Latina
PLS	Patrologia Latina, Supplementum
PSt	Patristic Studies, Washington, D. C.
SC	Sources chretiénnes
SCA	Studies in Christian Antiquity, Washington,D.C.
TU	Texte und Untersuchungen

Introduction

Because the Church is ultimately a mystery it cannot be defined. The writers of both Old and New Testaments help us to a sketchy understanding of its nature and purpose by a series of impressionistic figures or images which in turn are subjected to exegesis and illumination by the Fathers. John Chrysostom clearly understood this limitation of theological language in regard both to Christ and the Church. In one of his most dramatic preaching performances, his *Homily on the Fall of Eutropius*, he explains:

> Nothing is more abiding than the Church: she is your salvation; she is your refuge. She is more lofty than the heavens; she is more far-reaching than the earth. She never grows old; she always stays in bloom. And so Scripture indicates her permanence and stability by calling her a virgin; her magnificence by calling her a queen; her closeness to God by calling her a daughter; her barrenness turned to fecundity by calling her 'the mother of seven'. A thousand names try to spell out her nobility. Just as the Lord is called by many names — Father, Way, Life, Light, Arm, Propitation, Foundation, Gate, Sinless One, Treasure, Lord, God, Son, Only-Begotten, Form of God, Image of God —, since one name could not hope to describe the Omnipotent, and many names give us some small insight into His nature, so the Church goes by many names. (PG 52. 402)

Lumen Gentium reflects the same concern for description by resort to a multiplicity of images in its opening chapter. In the second chapter of *Lumen Gentium* the image of Church as the new People of God is dominant, which provides welcome complementary insights into the nature and mission of the Church. Again, Chrysostom, in the same homily, emphasizes the spiritual, rather than physical, nature of these images, and the fact that they are complementary, not contradictory:

> The church is many things: at one time a bride, at another a daughter, now a virgin, now a handmaid, now a queen; at one time barren, at another a garden; at one time fertile, at another a lily, at another a fountain. Therefore, when you hear these names beware of regarding them as physical.... A mountain is not a virgin, a virgin is not a bride, a queen is not a servant; yet the Church is all these things. Why? Because these are spiritual, not physical, realities, and the spiritual is a vast ocean.

The important principle established in Chapter Two is that when God devised a plan of salvation for mankind after the Fall He intended this plan to operate on a social rather than an individual basis, and because of this the chosen people of Israel, and later the new people of the Church, were given preferential status in the divine plan. Membership of the new People of God is acquired through baptism, and the Church, like Noah's Ark, becomes a necessary means of salvation.

One of the longest (some feel excessively long) chapters in *Lumen Gentium* is devoted to the Hierarchical Nature of the Church, mostly with the office of Pope and bishops, with relatively brief concluding sections on the priesthood and diaconate. The opening sections reiterate Vatican I teaching on the Petrine office, its primacy and infallibility, and the foundation by Christ of a college of apostles which transmitted its governing and teaching functions to the college of bishops. The newest perspective is the fullness of priesthood conferred in the sacramental ordination of bishops. The traditional stance on clerical celibacy is maintained, albeit not well attested in patristic teaching or practice. And there is no hint of the possibility of women becoming priests, although both these questions have come in for considerable scholarly debate in the two decades since the Council.

Chapter Four, on the Laity, emphasizes the fact that the call to sanctity goes out to clergy and laity alike, and that laity, like clergy, share in Christ's triple priestly, prophetic and kingly role. In virtue of this each lay person has the dignity of membership in the people of God and has a concomitant obligation to help extend Christ's Kingdom on earth by being an authentic witness to Christ's life, death and resurrection. Clergy and laity are seen to be complementary and integral segments of the one true Church.

Chapter Five more closely analyses the nature of holiness, its unity and diversity, and the means given us by Christ for authentic growth in holiness. Chapter Six, a logical consequence of the previous one, is devoted to Religious, who, from an early stage in the history of the Church, have sought perfection by embracing the evangelical counsels of chastity, poverty and obedience. The corresponding chapter in the present work will try to provide cameo studies of the rise and spread of monasticism, both Eastern and Western. Despite some regional differences in Egypt, Syria, Palestine, Cappadocia and Gaul this extraordinary quest of perfection will be seen to be remarkably homogeneous.

Early manifestations of anomianism in monasticism, together with bizarre manifestations of the prophetic and pneumatic role soon highlighted the need for some kind of hierarchical surveillance, so the correct relations between the monks and the hierarchy will receive due attention. Finally it will be emphasized that what began as a wholesale flight from the world did not, in fact, make monks antisocial, or impair their contributions to the social, economic and cultural life of the Church, or stunt the development of their own personalities. It might be noted here that the recent proliferation in scholarship prompted by the publication of the Coptic Nag-Hammadi documents — apparently the holdings of an early monastic library — tends to exaggerate early tensions between the monastic and hierarchical churches, even suggesting that the latter, the 'great' church, subjugated the former by questionable, forcible means with enormous resultant losses in genuine spirituality and the emergence of an overly-bureaucratic, all-male, hierarchical, pyramidical structure that was at variance with the simpler designs of the founder of Christianity. The 'evidence' advanced to support this tentative new history of the Church in the first three centuries is very frail and fragmentary, and need not be assumed to have seriously shaken the more traditional model of the early Church, one, holy, monastic and hierarchical.

Chapter Seven is devoted to the eschatological dimension of the Pilgrim Church, dealing with two other sections of the Church besides the Church militant on earth, namely the Church Triumphant in Heaven and the Church Suffering in Purgatory. This chapter on the Pilgrim Church emphasizes that only in the glory of Heaven will the Church attain its perfection but in the interim there is the possibility of a beneficial communication between the members of the church militant on earth and the church triumphant in Heaven. The Church's third constituency, namely souls undergoing purification in Purgatory, can be benefited by the intercessory prayers of the other two.

Chapter VIII, on Mary, provides an appropriate finale. One of the most enlightened perceptions of Vatican II was that it should not treat Ecclesiology and Mariology as separate subjects. The mother of the physical body of Christ was fittingly seen as the mother of His mystical body, the Church. She occupies a place in the Church which is the highest after Christ and yet very close to us.

The third century theologian and bishop, Hippolytus, although he wrote in Rome was from Asia Minor and was directly filiated through Irenaeus to John and his Apocalypse. When he comes to explain the woman clothed with the sun in chapter XII of the Apocalypse in his work *De Antichristo* this is what he says:

> 61 The Church never ceases to give birth to the Logos. 'And she brought forth a man-child to rule all nations' says the text: the perfect man that is Christ, the child of God, both God and man. And the Church brings forth this Christ when she teaches all nations. Admittedly, he is thinking about the Church, but his words can also apply to Mary.

A similar exegesis in Methodius also emphasizes that it is the Church that is being allegorized, but the fact that such emphasis is called for seems to indicate that the fashion of applying it to Mary was already prevalent.

> 8.3 Indeed this is she, our Mother, the great woman in heaven. This is the powerful heavenly archetype, greater than all her children. This is the Church; and her children, born through baptism in all parts of the world, die on the earth but rise and hasten to join their mother.... 8.5 My dear fault-finder, you yourself cannot prove that Christ Himself is the one that is brought forth (*Symposium*).

Ecclesiology in the Fathers

A diachronic view of the Fathers who will be quoted in the course of this work may be appropriate at this point. Among those known as the Apostolic Fathers we will have most frequent recourse to Clement of Rome (c.96) and Ignatius of Antioch (+107). The letters of Ignatius have been described as the epiphany of the monarchical episcopate and they will be especially cited in the third chapter on the Hierarchical Nature of the Church. *The Shepherd of Hermas*, in that it has been classified among the apocryphal apocalypses, requires more critical evaluation of its teaching on the Church. Its importance is that it may be the first authentically lay voice speaking on the church. The *Didache* may belong to early in the second century but because of the itinerant nature of the ministry which it seems to presuppose it may be representative of peripheral rather than mainline Church practice. It pioneered the way for later works like the *Didascalia of the Apostles* and *Constitutions of the Apostles*, and the *Apostolic Tradition* of Hippolytus of Rome (d. 235).

Among the Greek Apologists of the 2nd century we will often invoke Justin Martyr (d.c.165) and Melito of Sardis, as well as Theophilus of Antioch and Athenagoras of Athens. With the spread of Gnosticism in this century the anti-heretical writing of Irenaeus of Lyons provided a full-scale theology of the Church in its hierarchical constitution, and this receives corroboration in the East from what survives of the writings of Hegesippus in the *Ecclesiastical History* of Eusebius.

In the Latin West our first major witnesses for teaching on the Church are Tertullian (d. after 220), Novatian and Cyprian, bishop of Carthage during the stormy decade from 248 to 258, so poignantly overshadowed by the Decian persecution in 250.

Nowhere is Tertullian's ecclesiology so pervasive as in his anti-Marcionite work, *On the Prescription of Heretics*. Here he insists on the truth of all doctrine that comes through the Church from the apostles, but on the falsity of what is unsupported by apostolic tradition (c.21). The best indication of the fidelity of the tradition is the continuing identity of belief in churches which are widely separated geographically (c.28). In contrast with the teaching of the true church, the teaching of the heresies is relatively late (c.29). Based on the fact that truth is prior to falsehood (c.31) the heretics have no claim to the Scriptures which form a deposit of truth entrusted to, and carefully safe-guarded by, the true Church (c.37). With it, unlike the heretics, the Scriptures are maintained uncontaminated (c.38). Heretics prefer to subvert than to convert, to pull down rather than to build. In a word, 'all heresies, when thoroughly looked into, are detected harboring dissent in many particulars, even from their own founders. The majority of them have not even churches. Motherless, houseless, creedless outcasts, they wander about in their own essential worthlessness' (c.42).

Tertullian, although born in Carthage, had been trained

in Rome, with special attention to rhetoric and law, and became a convert there. For about a decade after his return to Carthage he used his considerable literary talents in the service of the Church, but unfortunately around 207 he defected to Montanism as a protest against the alleged laxity of the Catholic Church and he died a Montanist around 220.

Cyprian was also a native of Carthage and also came to the Church as a convert and from a rhetorical training. Among his various treatises the most important for our purposes is, undoubtedly, *On the Unity of the Church*. His insistence on the need for Church membership is summed up in his adage: He cannot have God for his Father who has not any longer Church for his mother (*On the Unity of the Church*, 6).

Cyprian's Letters are a goldmine of information on the Church at Carthage around the middle of the 3rd century. In Letter 1 he reminds the priests, deacons and people of Furni in Tunisia that the priesthood is a full-time job: 'everyone honored by the divine priesthood and consecrated for the clerical ministry ought only to serve the altar and the sacrifices, and to have time for prayers and petitions.' He shows his practical concern for the poor in Letter 7: 'I request you diligently to care for the widows and the infirm and all the poor. Moreover, you may furnish to itinerants, if any should be indigent, expenses from my own portion.' He shows his willingness to consult with his priests and people in ep. 14: 'from the beginning of my episcopate I decided to do nothing of my own opinion privately without your advice and the consent of the people.' In ep. 17 he promises that 'when, after peace has first been restored to us all by the Lord, we shall begin to return to the Church, each one will be examined in your presence and with you judging.'

But, in the ongoing exchanges with the Lapsed, he makes clear who speaks for the Church and who does not: 17.2 I hear that some of the priests, not mindful of the Gospel, not considering what the martyrs have written to us, not reserving to the bishop the honor of his priesthood and his see, have already begun to be in communion with the lapsed and to offer for them the Sacrifice and to give them the Eucharist although they should come to these things in due order... no one can come to Communion unless first hands have been imposed on him by the bishop and the clergy.

Novatian was the first theologian in Rome to write in Latin, and became a priest, so Eusebius tells us (h.e. V1.43), 'against the opposition of all the clergy as well as of many laymen. After an exchange of letters with Cyprian (cf. epp. 30, 36 in *Novatian*, FOTC 67.187-204) on the correct procedure in the re-admission of the Lapsed he gradually went from a policy of leniency to a complete break with the Church of Rome, setting himself up as an anti-Pope and head of a rigorist sect called the Novatianists, or 'the pure ones' (Gk. *katharoi*, cf. the later Catharists). They excluded from their membership not only those who had lapsed in the persecution but also anyone guilty of mortal sin. And they considered as invalid even the baptism of Catholics, requiring converts to Novatianism to be re-baptized.

The two great Alexandrians of the early 3rd century — Clement (d. before 215) and Origen (d.253) — are important for their rejection of pagan mythology and systematic exposition of the shortcomings of Greek philosophy. Clement's most important works — the *Protrepticus*, the *Paidagogos* and the *Stromata* — are continuously preoccupied with the stark contrasts between the old, pagan, and the new, Christian worlds. In *Paid.* 1.7.42 Clement says: 'There is only one virginal mother: I will call her the Church.' And in *Stromata* V1. 107 the three-fold ecclesiastical hierarchy is seen to be modelled on the angelic hierarchy.

For Clement of Alexandria the Church is the new people of God: 'Then the new people, in contrast to the older people, are young, because they have heard the new good things.... For those who have partaken of the new Word must be themselves new. But whatever partakes of eternity assumes, by that very fact, the qualities of the incorruptible; therefore the name 'childhood' is for us a life-long springtime, because the truth abiding in us is ageless, and our being, made to overflow with that truth is ageless too.... A mother draws her children near her; we seek our mother, the

Church' (*Paid*.1.5,20-21). Elsewhere he clearly teaches that the Church is the body of Christ, nourished on His body and blood (*Paid.* 1.6.42).

Origen, however, is the unrivalled intellectual giant of the period. Despite his enormous literary output it is noticeable that he never gave an extended treatment of ecclesiology in any single place. But he frequently gives us passing insights on the nature and destiny of the Church and his own proudest boast is to be an 'ecclesiastical' man. A typical statement of his can be quoted from his *Commentary on the Canticle of Canticles:* 'I would not have you suppose that the 'bride of Christ' or the Church is spoken of only after the coming of the Saviour in the flesh: but rather from the beginning of the human race, from the very foundation of the world; rather, I would follow St. Paul in tracing the origin of this mystery even further, before the foundation of the world.' And, in his *Homilies on Leviticus* he shows his high regard for the priesthood: 'For in the ordination of a priest the presence of the people is also required, that all may know for certain that the man elected to priesthood is a man of the whole people the most eminent, the most learned, the holiest, the most outstanding in every virtue.' (SC 286.279).

Methodius (+311) was an early adversary of Origen. Here we will sometimes invoke his *Banquet, or On Virginity*, especially for its vivid imagery in describing the Church. Typical of his approach is the following: 'Thus the prophetic word can compare the Church with a meadow full of gay-colored flowers, adorned and garlanded not only with the blossoms of chastity but also with those of continence and motherhood: for on the right hand of the Bridegroom stands the Queen ornate in a gold-embroidered gown' (cf. Ps. 44: 10,14, Discourse 2, ACW 27. 57, tr. H. Musurillo). This is very similar to a very famous and very early inscription, datable to the end of the 2nd century and found in Phrygia. It is known as the inscription of Abercius and reads in part: 'Abercius by name, I am a disciple of the chaste shepherd, who feeds his flocks on the mountains and plains, who has great eyes that look out on all sides. He taught me...faithful writings. He sent me to Rome, to behold a kingdom and to see a queen with golden robe and golden shoes. There I saw a people bearing the splendid seal'. Clearly, Christ is the shepherd, the queen is the Church, and the seal is baptism.

Hippolytus is one of the least well-known of the Fathers despite his considerable literary legacy. Less than seventy years after his death the historian Eusebius was not sure what see in the East he headed (h.e.V1.20). In his numerous works of exegesis he displays a marked fondness for allegory and he frequently discovers images of the New Covenant in many unpromising texts in the Old Testament. In his *Commentary on Daniel,* for instance, the episode of an unsuspecting Susanna walking in the garden under the surveillance of the two lusty elders undergoes a completely ecclesial metamorphosis (cf.Dan.13:1-64). Both Susanna and the garden become figures of the Church. Babylon is the world and the two elders are figures of persecution while Susanna's husband, Joachim, is a figure of Christ. The garden scene reminds Hippolytus of the text in Galatians: 'some who do not really belong to the brotherhood have furtively crept in to spy on the liberty we enjoy in Christ Jesus' (Gal. 2:4). The hot day on which Susanna wanted to bathe in the garden (Dan. 13:15) is the day of the Pasch. That is the day on which the bath that refreshes is prepared in the garden; the Church, bathed like Susanna, stands like a pure bride before God. Even the oil and balsam (Dan. 13:17) assume baptismal associations.

Elsewhere in the same *Commentary* we are told that the Church is not called a place or a house built of stone or clay; it can no longer be called an isolated person, for houses are destroyed and men die. Rather, the Church is the sacred union of those who live in justice. Concord, the path of the saints toward the community — that is what it is, the spiritual garden of God, planted in Eden.

Lactantius at the beginning of the 4th century is a sort of Latin counterpart to Origen's *First Principles* in his work called *Divine Institutes.* He displays wide knowledge of the Latin classics, especially Cicero, in outlining the superiority of Christianity to paganism. As a tutor at the court of

Diocletian he himself had converted to Christianity during the persecution. He is one of our best historical sources for the history of the various persecutions against the church in his *On the Death of the Persecutors.*

The Golden Age of Greek Patristic literature extends from Athanasius of Alexandria, the resolute opponent of Arius (256-336), to Theodoret, bishop of Cyrus, outside Antioch (393-458). Besides his various refutations of Arianism and his extensive volume of letters that survive, Athanasius is instructive for us here in his *Life of Antony*, a most important document in the history of earliest monasticism. This work, as well as the writings of such early monks as Pachomius, Evagrius and Macarius, will be used in the chapter on Religious. Cyril was a distinguished successor of Athanasius in the see of Alexandria. He presided over the Council of Ephesus (431) and was largely responsible for restoring the title *Theotokos*, Mother of God, to the Blessed Virgin Mary against the machinations of Nestorius.

The three great Cappadocian Fathers — Basil (330-379), Gregory Nazianzus (330-390) and Gregory of Nyssa (335-394) will frequently be quoted, especially their letters, to illustrate episcopal collegiality in action in the 4th century. Eusebius of Caesarea will also be frequently resorted to, especially his *Ecclesiastical History*, to provide some historical framework, though it should be borne in mind that he is frequently accused of seeing the 2nd century Church through 4th century contact lenses.

The ever-widening outreach of the Roman primate can be easily illustrated from the letters of Leo the Great, bishop of Rome, 440-461. His first letter, to the bishop of Aquileia, complains of certain priests, deacons, and people in minor orders, who have succumbed to the Pelagian heresy 'while the shepherds, set to watch, were fast asleep'. He tells Dioscorus, bishop of Alexandria, that the two of them should be one in thought and act (cf. Acts 4:32), and invokes history to reinforce his point: since the most blessed Peter received the headship of the apostles from the Lord, and the church of Rome still abides by his decrees, it is malicious to suppose that the holy disciple, Mark, who was the first to govern the

church of Alexandria, formed his decrees on a different line
of tradition (ep.9). Epistle 12, addressed to all the bishops of
the province of Mauritania Caesariensis in Africa, seeks to
check their irregularities in the choice and ordination of
bishops, especially in premature promotions. It includes an
illuminating directive on not multiplying episcopal sees
beyond necessity: Bishops should not be consecrated in any
place or in any hamlet where they have not been consecrated
before; for where the flocks are small, the care of the presbyters may suffice, whereas the episcopal authority ought to
preside only over larger flocks and more crowded cities, lest,
contrary to the divinely-inspired decrees of the holy
Fathers, the priestly office be assigned over villages and
rural estates or obscure and thinly-populated townships,
and the position of honor, to which only the more important
charges should be given, be held cheap from the very
number of those who hold it. (PL 54.654).

Donatism originated in Africa during the Diocletian persecution, in 311, when Donatus, bishop of Numidia at the
head of a party of fanatical Christians refused to recognize
Cecilian, the lawfully consecrated bishop of Carthage. The
pretext was that the latter had been consecrated by *tradi-
tores*, that is, bishops who had handed over the sacred
books into the hands of the persecutors. Donatus himself
soon became bishop of Carthage and gave his name to the
new sect, which quickly spread to neighboring dioceses
throughout Africa. The chief defender of orthodoxy against
the Donatists was Augustine, who wrote a series of anti-
Donatist tracts, dealing with the nature and distinguishing
marks of the true Church. The Donatists felt that they alone
had been uncontaminated by sin and so were the sole bene-
factors of the true Church. They questioned the validity of
sacraments administered by their opponents.

Augustine began from the principle that sanctity could be
found only in the one, true Church, but he denied that
sanctity was the prerogative of a Church that insisted on
being something exclusive, already perfect, and dependent
for the propagation of sanctity to its members on the sanctity of the ministers of the sacraments. For Augustine a

sacrament is as much a sign of religious union and community as of the sanctification of the individual. The Church herself, he saw as a sort of super-sacrament, a visible sign of visible communion with Christ.

Optatus, bishop of Mileve in Numidia tried to mediate the dispute and moderate the fanaticism of the Donatists by writing an elaborate work called *Against Parmenianus the Donatist,* to which he added *A Collection of Documents relating to the Donatist Controversy.*

The ecclesiology of Augustine of Hippo is a synthesis of *Lumen Gentium*, and vice-versa. He frequently thinks of the Church in figures and types, beginning with Eve: '...why did he sleep? Because Adam was the figure of the one to come, and Adam slept when Eve was made out of his side. Adam, the figure of Christ, Eve, the figure of the Church, whence she was called the mother of the living. When was Eve fashioned? While Adam slept. When did the sacraments of the Church flow from the side of Christ? When He slept on the cross' (*Enarr. in ps*.40, 10, CSEL 38.456). In his lengthy *On Baptism, against the Donatists* he elaborates his teaching on the necessity of membership of the People of God achieved through baptism. The baptism of the gentile Cornelius by Peter (cf. Acts 10:45-48) provides Scriptual warrant on the exclusivity of baptism and its necessity (*De bapt.c.Don.*, 1.VIII,10, CSEL 51.155), and the Ark is the symbol of salvation: 'As it was not another but the same water that saved those who were placed within the ark, and destroyed those who were without the ark, so it is not by different baptisms but by the same that good Catholics are saved and bad Catholics or heretics perish' (op.cit.5.XX-VIII,39,CSEL 51.297).

The one true Church, for Augustine, is above all else the sure bulwark against heresy and the guarantor of the purity of the transmission of Scripture and Tradition: 'This same is the holy Church, the one Church, the true Church, the catholic Church, fighting against all heresies; it is capable of fighting, but incapable of being vanquished. Heresies all went out of it like unprofitable branches pruned from the vine; it abides itself in its Vine, in its charity'(On the Creed, a

Sermon to Catechumens, PL 40.635).

The common bond is charity: 'Let us love our Lord, God, let us love His Church: Him as a Father, Her as a Mother: Him as a Lord, Her as His Handmaid, as we are ourselves the Handmaid's sons. But this marriage is held together by a bond of great love; no one offends the one, and wins favor with the other.... Hold, then, most beloved, hold all with one mind to God the Father and the Church our Mother' (*Enarr. in Ps. 88*, PL 37.1140).

The following illustrates the eloquent testimony of St. Augustine to the nature and dignity of the Church of his day:

> There are many other things which keep me in the bosom of the Catholic Church. The consent of peoples and nations keeps me, her authority keeps me, inaugurated by miracles, nourished in hope, enlarged by love, and established by age. The succession of priests keeps me, from the very seat of the Apostle Peter (to whom the Lord after His resurrection gave charge to feed His sheep) down to the present episcopate. And so, lastly, does the name of Catholic itself, which not without reason, amid so many heresies, the Church has alone retained; so that though all heretics wish to be called Catholics, yet, when a stranger asks where the Church is, no heretic will dare to point to his own chapel or house. Such in number and importance are the precious ties belonging to the christian name which keep a believer in the Catholic Church. (Contra Ep. Manichaei, 4,5, PL 42.175).

In an article entitled "Vatican II: The Hidden Question" in *Doctrine and Life* (January, 1983), Noel Dermot O'Donoghue writes: What then of Vatican II? What question did it pose and how was/is this question related to the Hidden Question? Obviously it posed many questions, and provided many answers.... It is generally agreed, however, that the central question of the Council was that of the nature of the Church. But it was posed no longer precisely in terms of nature and definition, but in terms of mystery and exploration. This approach, sometimes rather vaguely called existential, was quite new, disconcertingly so for those trained in the old school of question and answer, of definite and definable essences.

In a similar spirit the present volume will present quotations from the Fathers not so much in terms of nature and definition of the Church but rather in terms of mystery and exploration. All too often in the past the Fathers were ransacked by theologians for quotations to bolster the current view on a particular subject rather than to find out what the Fathers themselves had to say. Here, the focus will be on how the Fathers envisioned their Church, but there will be no effort to portray a church, yesterday, today and the same forever. The paragraph divisions will follow those of *Lumen Gentium* and, while patristic citations in the Council document will in general be presented, other texts will sometimes be introduced to show a certain diversity in early church belief and practice. The totality, it is hoped, will give an accurate picture of the general lineaments of the Church of the first five centuries.

I

The Mystery of the Church

CHRIST, LIGHT OF THE WORLD

#1 Christ is the light of humanity...proclaiming his Gospel to every creature may bring to all men that light of Christ which shines out visibly from the Church.

One of the earliest statements of Christ as the light of the world is found in the *Epistle to the Ephesians* of Ignatius of Antioch. Because of its poetical character, some scholars regard it as a pre-Ignatian hymn, utilized by Ignatius to provide a memorable summary to the main themes in his letter:

> 19[1]...A star shone in heaven,
> brighter than all the other stars,
> and its brightness was indescribable,
> and its unusualness caused a strange wonder;
> And the other stars, and sun, and moon,
> danced in chorus about the star,
> but it was radiating its light
> far beyond the others.
> The wonder grew
> what made it new,
> so unlike the entire chorus.
> From then all magic was destroyed,

[1]Text: SC 10.88

and every shackle of sin was abolished;
ignorance was scattered,
and the ancient kingdom was ruined,
when God incarnate appeared
to bring newness of eternal life (cf.Rom.6:4).
What had been decided by God
began to be realized:
and because of the plan for abolishing death
all things were in motion.

The hymn is obviously inspired by the appearance of the star to the Magi, the *Lumen Gentium*, or Light of the Gentiles.

Also in the second century, from an anonymous author in Asia Minor,[2] we have a paschal homily saying much the same thing:

Now is the time when the blessed light of Christ sheds its rays; the pure rays of the pure Spirit rise and the heavenly treasures of divine glory are opened up. Night's darkness and obscurity have been swallowed up and the dense blackness dispersed in this light of day; crabbed death has been totally eclipsed. Life has been extended to every creature and all things are diffused in brightness. The dawn of dawn ascends over the earth and "He who was before the morning star" (Ps.109,2) and before the other stars, the mighty Christ, immortal and all powerful, sheds light brighter than the sun on the universe.

For all of us his faithful He has initiated a bright, new day, long, eternal, and unquenchable; it is the mystical Pasch, celebrated in figures under the Law but fulfilled in very truth by Christ; the marvellous Pasch, the wonder of divine virtue, the work of power, truly a feast, an everlasting memorial, impassibility born of suffering, immortality born of death, life born in the tomb, healing born from wounds, resurrection born from the fall, ascent to Heaven born from descent to Hell.

[2]Text: SC 27.117 ed. Nautin

Christ the light of all nations, the *Lumen Gentium* was dramatised for Christians during the paschal vigil, vividly described for us by Gregory of Nyssa in a paschal homily:[3]

> What have we seen? A light like a cloud of fire of the candles burning throughout the night. All night our ears have resounded with psalms, hymns and spiritual canticles; it was like a river of joy running through our ears to our soul and filling us with blessed hopes. And our heart, delighted by what we heard and saw, was marked with ineffable joy, conducting us by means of the visible spectacle to the invisible. Those blessings "which eye has not seen, nor ear heard, nor have entered into the heart of men" (1 Cor. 2:9) are shown to us in replica by the blessings of this day of rest. They are a guarantee for us of the ineffable blessings we hope for.
>
> Since, then, this night is aglow with lights, in which the brightness of the lights is intermingled with the first streaks of dawn making one day without any interval of darkness, let us reflect, brethren, on the prophecy that says: "This is the day which the Lord has made "(Ps. 118:24). This proposes to us nothing difficult or hard, but joy, happiness, rejoicing, since it goes on to say: "Let us rejoice and be glad in it". O wonderful instruction! O sweet command! Who can be slow to carry out such instructions? Who does not feel guilty at even a slight postponement in carrying out these orders? Joy is our task; we are instructed to rejoice. By this the judgment pronounced on sin is effaced and grief is turned into joy.

The Church is explicitly spoken of as a sacrament by Firmilian in a letter to Cyprian:

> 75.15.[4] But neither must we pass over what has necessarily being said by you, that the Church, according to the Canticle of Canticles, is a garden enclosed and a fountain sealed, a paradise with the fruit of apple trees. But they who have never entered into this garden and have not

---

[3]Text: PG 46.681   [4]Text: CSEL 3,2,820

seen the Paradise planted by God the Creator, how can they offer to anyone the living water of the salutary washing from the fountain which is enclosed within and is sealed with the divine seal?

And since, in truth, the ark of Noah was nothing else but the sacrament of the Church of Christ, which then saved only those who were within the ark, whereas all without were perishing, clearly we are instructed to have regard for the unity of the Church as Peter has stated (cf. 1 Pet. 3:20), — so also baptism will save us likewise showing that just as those who were not with Noah in the ark were not cleansed and sanctified by the water, but immediately perished in that flood, so now also whoever are not in the Church with Christ will perish without, unless they are converted to the only and life-giving font of the Church through penance.

THE PRE-EXISTENCE OF THE CHURCH

#2 *He determined to call together in a holy Church those who should believe in Christ. Already present in figure at the beginning of the world, this Church was prepared in marvellous fashion in the history of the people of Israel and in the old Alliance.*

The notions of prior type in the Old Covenant and full realization in the New are very fundamental to an understanding of the idea that the history of the Church extends from the beginning to the end of time. This is how Ignatius describes this lengthy genealogy:[5]

> With heartiest good wishes for good for unalloyed joy in Jesus Christ to the church at Ephesus in Asia Minor, a church deserving of felicitation blessed as she is with greatness through the fulness of the Father; predestined before time was to be, to her abiding and changeless glory, forever united and chosen through real suffering by the will of the Father.

[5]Text: SC 10.56

All the elect, before time began, the Father *foreknew and predestined to become conformed to the image of His Son, that He should be the firstborn among many brethren* (Rom. 8:29).

The pre-existence of the Church is a distinctive teaching of Jewish Christianity. It is clearly found in Vision 11 of *The Shepherd of Hermas*, where the handsome young man tells Hermas more about the elderly lady who featured in Vision 1. He identifies her as 'the Church', and she is elderly 'because she was created first of all; that is why she is elderly, and for her the world was made'.

The teaching is also found in one of the newly-found Gnostic discoveries *Treatise of the Three Natures*, which speaks of 'the Church which exists before the aeons', and the Gnostic, Theodotus, in Clement of Alexandria's *Excerpta*, 41 speaks of 'the Church, chosen before the foundation of the world'. Elsewhere, in his *Protrepticus*, Clement explains the concept of 'first-born church' at greater length:

> IX.82[6] Come, come, young people! *For if you do not become again as little children, and be born again,* as the Scripture says, *you shall not receive the truly existent Father, (cf.Mt.18:3). and you shall never enter into the kingdom of heaven.* Now in what way is a stranger permitted to enter? As I see it, at the point when he is enrolled and becomes a citizen, and receives one to take the place of a father in relation to him, then the Father's concerns will become his own, then he shall be deemed worthy to be made his heir, then will he share the Father's Kingdom with his dearly-beloved Son.
>
> For this is the first-born Church, composed of many good children; these are the first-born enrolled in Heaven, who hold high festival with so many myriads of angels. We too are first-born sons, who are reared by God, who are the genuine friends of the first-born, who first and foremost attained to the knowledge of God.

[6]Text: SC 2.149

The so-called Second Epistle of Clement has a remarkable passage in which the Church is represented as existing before the sun and moon, when she was invisible and barren, but she is now the incarnate Body of Christ, bride and mother:

> XIV[7] So, then, brethren, if we do the will of our Father, God, we shall be members of the first church, the spiritual — that which was created before the sun and moon. But if we shall not do the will of the Lord we shall incur the Scripture which says: My house has become a den of thieves (cf. Mt.21:13). Therefore let us choose to belong to the Church of life, that we may be saved. But I do not think that you are ignorant that the living Church is the body of Christ. For the Scriptures say: God made them male and female (Gen.1:27). The male is Christ, the female is the Church. And besides, the Books (i.e. the Old Testament) and the Apostles say that the Church is not of the present but has been from the very beginning. For she was spiritual as was also our Jesus, but He was manifested in the last days that He might save us. Now the Church, being spiritual, was manifested in the flesh of Christ, thereby showing us that if anyone of us guard her in the flesh and defile her not, he shall receive her back again in the Holy Spirit. . . . Now if we say that the flesh is the Church and the Spirit is Christ, then in truth he who has dishonored the flesh has dishonored the Church. Such a one shall not, therefore, partake of the Spirit, which is Christ.

The account in Genesis XXVII of Rebecca substituting her younger son, Jacob for the elder son, Esau, to receive the blessing of their dying father, Isaac, is used by many of the Fathers as an image of the synagogue and the church. Thus Ambrose, in *Jacob and the Happy Life*, writes:

---

[7]Text: LCL, *The Apostolic Fathers*, v.1, ed. Lake, 150

2.2.9[8] Accordingly, Jacob received his brother's clothing (cf.Gen.27:15) because he excelled his brother in wisdom... Rebecca presented this clothing as a symbol of the Church; she gave to the younger son the clothing of the Old Testament, the prophetic and priestly clothing, the royal Davidic clothing, the clothing of Kings Solomon, Ezechias and Josias, and she gave it too to the Christian people, who would know how to use the garment they had received, since the Jewish people kept it without using it and did not know its proper adornments. This clothing was lying in a shadow, cast off and forgotten; it was disfigured by a deep haze of impiety and could not be unfolded further in their narrow hearts. The Christian people put it on and it became resplendent. They made it shine with the brightness of their faith and the light of their good works. Isaac recognized the familiar fragrance that attached to his people; he recognized the clothing of the Old Testament, but he no longer recognized the voice of the people of old. Accordingly he knew that it had been changed. Even today the same clothing remains but the confession of a people of greater devotion resounds harmoniously; Isaac was right to say: "The voice is the voice of Jacob, but the hands are the hands of Esau" (Gen. 27:22).

There is a good statement of this important historical phenomenon in the *Symposium* of Methodius:

9.2[9] For the Law is a shadow and type of the image, that is to say of the Gospel; and the image, the Gospel represents the Truth which will be fulfilled at the second Coming of Christ. Thus the ancients and the Law foretold to us and prophesied the features of the Church, and the Church foretells those of the new order.

And we, who have accepted the Christ who said, *I am the Truth*, realize that the shadows and types have come to an end and *we press on towards the truth*, proclaiming

[8]Text: CSEL 32,2.36: CF. FOTC 65. 150, tr, M.P. McHugh
[9]Text: SC 95.268

it in vivid images. For as of now *we know in part* and, so
to speak, *through a glass*, for *that which is perfect* is not
yet come to us, the kingdom of heaven and the resurrection, when *that which is in part shall be taken away.*

On that day our tabernacles will be established, when
our bodies rise again, their bones once again fixed and
compacted with flesh. Then we shall celebrate to the Lord
the day of joy in a pure fashion, receiving at last eternal
tabernacles, never more destined to die or to dissolution
into the clay of the grave.

Origen speaks of the Church as a bride and as pre-existent
in his *Commentary on the Canticle of Canticles*:

> 11.8[10] Do not believe that the Bride, that is, the Church,
> has existed only since the Savior's Incarnation. She exists
> since the beginning of the human race and even since the
> creation of the world; even, as St. Paul testifies, since
> before the creation of the world. (cf.Eph.1:4) So the
> Church's foundations have been laid from the beginning.

Augustine sees three stages in the life of the Church — the
Church from Abel, the Church from Abraham, and the
Church here and now. In his *Enarrations on the Psalms* he is
even more detailed:

> 128.2[11] The Church is of ancient birth. Since saints have
> been so called the Church has been on earth. At one time
> the Church was in Abel only...at one time in Enoch
> alone...at one time in the house of Noah alone...at one
> time...in Abraham alone.

And in *The City of God*:

> XVIII.51[12] In evil days like these the Church walks on-
> ward like a wayfarer stricken by the world's hostility, but
> comforted by the mercy of God. Nor does this state of
> affairs date only from the days of the presence of Christ

[10]Text: PG 13.134; cf. ACW 26.149, tr. R. P. Lawson
[11]Text: CCL 40.3, 1882   [12]Text: CSEL 40.353

and His Apostles on earth. It was never any different from the days when the first just man, Abel, was slain by his ungodly brother. So it shall be until this world is no more.

Leo the Great puts the matter in succinct, almost juridical, terms:

30.7[13] All the saints who preceded the time of Our Savior were justified by this faith and were made the body of Christ by this sacrament, awaiting the universal redemption of the faithful.

Gregory the Great goes into more detail in his *Homilies on the Gospels*:[14]

h.19 In the reading of the holy Gospel much elucidation is required which I wish, if I may, to deal with summarily lest I burden you with unduly long and prolix exposition. The kingdom of Heaven is said to resemble a property owner who brought hired workmen to tend his vineyard. Who more closely resembles this vineyard owner than the Creator who rules his creatures and possesses his elect in this world as a master does his slaves in his household — the vineyard owner, that is the universal church, which from Abel the just to the last chosen one who will be born at the end of the world. The Church produces as many saints as the vineyard shoots. The owner of the vineyard brings workers to cultivate it at dawn, and at the third, sixth, ninth and eleventh hours, because from the beginning of the world to the end he does not cease to assemble preachers for the instruction of the people, his faithful. For the dawn of the world was from Adam to Noah, the third hour from Noah to Abraham, the sixth hour from Abraham to Moses, the ninth hour from Moses to the coming of the Lord, the eleventh hour from the coming of the Lord to the end of the world.

[13]Text: SC 22².198, ed. Leclerca-Dolle.   [14]Text: PL 76.1154

The same point is made by Caesarius of Arles:

> s.139[15] The Catholic Church was not only preached after the coming of our Lord and Savior, beloved brethren, but from the beginning of the world, it was designated by many figures and rather hidden mysteries. Indeed, in holy Abel the Catholic Church existed, in Noe, in Abraham, in Isaac, in Jacob, and in the other saintly people before the advent of our Lord and Savior.

Elsewhere, in sermon 12, he gives the biblical basis for this by quoting Heb. 11:6, *By faith Abel, by faith Henoch, by faith Noe, by faith Abraham pleased God.*

CHRIST AND THE CHURCH

#3 *To carry out the will of the Father Christ inaugurated the kingdom of heaven on earth and revealed to us his mystery; by his obedience, He brought about our redemption. The Church-that is, the kingdom of Christ, already present in mystery, grows visibly through the power of God in the world.*

St. John Chrysostom, commenting on the text: "And undoubtedly great is the mystery of piety; God Who was manifest in the flesh justified in the Spirit" (1 Tim.3:16), says:

> XI.[16] Here He speaks of the Dispensation in our behalf. Do not tell me of the bells, or of the holy of holies, or of the high priest. The Church is the pillar of the world. Consider this mystery and you will be awe-stricken: for it is indeed 'a great mystery' and a 'mystery of piety' and it is 'undoubtedly great' because it is beyond question. Since in his direction to the priests he had stipulated nothing like the regulations in Leviticus he refers the whole matter to a Higher Being, saying, "God was manifest in the

[15]Text: CCL 103. 571   [16]Text: PG 62.554

flesh." The Creator appeared incarnate. He was "justified in the Spirit." As it was written, "Wisdom is justified by her children," or because He practised no guile as the prophet says, "Because he has done no violence, neither was guile found in his mouth" (Isa. 53:9). He was "seen of angels". Angels together with us saw the Son of God, not having seen Him before. Great, truly great, was this mystery.

The dispensation on our behalf he calls a mystery, and well may it be called so, since it is not manifest to all. Indeed it was not manifest to the angels, for how could it, since 'it was made known by the Church' (Eph. 3:10)? Therefore he says, "Undoubtedly, great is the mystery of piety." Great indeed it was. For God became man, and man became God.

THE HOLY SPIRIT AND THE CHURCH

#4 *The Holy Spirit was sent on the day of Pentecost in order that he might continually sanctify the Church, and that, consequently, those who believe might have access through Christ in one Spirit to the Father.*

Irenaeus, in his *Against the Heresies*, describes the place of the Holy Spirit in the Church:

> 3.24[17] We receive our faith from the Church and keep it safe; and it is a precious deposit stored in a fine vessel, ever renewing its vitality through the Spirit of God, and causing the renewal of the vessel in which it is stored. For the gift of God has been entrusted to the Church, as the breath of life to created man, that all members by receiving it should be made alive. And herein has been bestowed on us our means of communion with Christ, namely the Holy Spirit, the pledge of immortality, the strengthening of our faith, the ladder by which we ascend to God. For the Apostle says, "God has set up in the

[17]Text: SC 34.398

Church apostles, prophets, teachers " (1 Cor.12:28) and all the other means of the Spirit's workings. But they have no share in this Spirit who do not join in the activity of the Church. . . . For where the Church is, there is the Spirit of God, and where the Spirit of God is, there is the Church and every kind of grace. The Spirit is truth. Therefore those who have no share in the Spirit are not nourished and given life at their mother's breast; nor do they enjoy the sparkling fountain that issues from the body of Christ.

By the power of the Gospel He (the Spirit) makes the Church grow, perpetually renews her, and leads her to perfect union with Her Spouse.

There are many descriptions in the Fathers of the early providential spread of the Church throughout the world. Lactantius, in the *Divine Institutes*, is typical:

> IV.[18] After His preaching of the Gospel and His Name to the disciples was completed, He withdrew Himself suddenly, and the clouds took Him into Heaven on the fortieth day after His Passion, just as Daniel had revealed would happen, saying: *One like the Son of Man coming in the clouds of heaven. And he came even to the ancient of days* (Dan. 7:13).
>
> His disciples, however, dispersing through the provinces, made foundations of the churches everywhere, and they performed great, almost incredible miracles, in the name of God, their Master. For as He was about to depart He instructed them in the virtue and power, whereby the plan of the new message might be established and confirmed. And He also made known to them all that would take place.

At this point Lactantius introduces a long quotation from the apocryphal *Preaching of Peter and Paul*:

[18]Text:CSEL 19.367; cf. E.Hennecke, *New Testament Apocrypha*, tr.R.McL.Wilson, 2, Philadelphia, 1976, 93.

Peter had preached these things in Rome, and that preaching has remained in writing as a testimony to them. In this they have recorded both many other wonders and that this also would take place, that after a brief interval God would send a ruler who would attack the Jews and raze their cities to the ground, and lay siege to them after they had been ravaged by hunger and thirst. The outcome would be that they would cannibalistically feed on their own bodies and, finally captured, would fall into the hands of the enemy. And in their sight they would behold their own wives most bitterly attacked, virgins violated, their youths deported.

Thus the Church shines forth as "a people made one with the unity of the Father, the Son, and the Holy Spirit".

This, one of the explicit quotations from the Fathers in *Lumen Gentium* is from Cyprian, *On the Lord's Prayer*, 23 (CCL IIIA.105). Similar sentiments can be found in Augustine and Cyril of Alexandria. To take Cyril first, quoting from his *Commentary on John*:

XI.II[19] (Commenting on Jn. 17: 20-21)
Christ is taking the substantial unity which He has with the Father and the Father with Him as an image or model of that indestructible love, harmony and unity which obtains where there is real and deep concord. He thus indicates His wish that in the strength of the holy and substantial Trinity, we too should be commingled with one another, so that the whole body of the Church may be perceived as one, as moving in Christ, through the union of two peoples, towards the constitution of a perfect, single whole. This is what St. Paul says: *For He is our peace, who has made the two one and in his own body of flesh and blood has broken down the dividing wall of hostility, by abolishing in his flesh the law of commandments and ordinances, that He might create in himself*

[19] Text: PG 74.556

one new man in place of the two, so making peace, and might reconcile both to God in one body through the cross, bringing the hostility to an end (Eph. 2:14-16).

St. Augustine stresses the role of the Church in achieving unity and reconciliation:

> s. 71.20[20] The remission of sins, since it cannot be given without the Holy Spirit can only be granted in the church. Peter said: Do penance and be baptized, each one of you, in the name of Jesus Christ, that your sins may be forgiven; then you will receive that gift of the Holy Spirit. (Acts 2:37-38). Both, therefore, were done in the church, that is, both the remission of sins and the reception of this Gift, in which the Holy Spirit resided.

THE FOUNDATION OF THE CHURCH

#5 *The mystery of the Church is already brought to light in the way it was founded. For the Lord Jesus inaugurated his Church by preaching the Good News, that is the coming of the kingdom of God. The Church... receives the mission of proclaiming and establishing among all peoples the kingdom.*

Irenaeus virtually draws a map for us to illustrate the catholicity of the church of his day. In the *Against the Heresies* he says:

> 1.10.2[21]Neither do the churches in Germany believe any differently, or transmit the faith any differently, nor those in Iberia, nor among the Celts, nor in the East, nor in Egypt, nor in Libya, nor in the centre of the world (i.e. Jerusalem); but just as the sun, the creation of God, is one and the same all over the world, so also the light, the proclamation of the truth, shines forth everywhere, and

[20]Text: PL 38.463   [21]Text: SC 264,158

illuminates all men who wish to come to a knowledge of the truth.

Likewise Tertullian from his vantage point in North Africa:[22]

> For whose right hand does God the Father hold but that of Christ, His Son whom all nations have heard, that is, whom all nations have believed? His preachers, the apostles, are pointed to in the Psalms of David, who says: Into the universal earth has gone forth their sound, and unto the ends of the earth their voice. (Ps. 18:5)
>
> For in whom else has the universe of nations believed except in the Christ who has already come? For whom have the nations believed-Parthians, Medes, Elamites, the inhabitants of Mesopotamia, Armenia, Phrygia, Cappadocia, they who dwell in Pontus, Asia Minor, Pamphylia, occupants of Egypt, of the region of Africa beyond Cyrene, Romans and sojourners, yes, and in Jerusalem, Jews and all other nations, for example, by this time, the varied races of the Getulians, and numerous regions of the Moors, all the territories of the Spains, and the different tribes of the Gauls, of the Sarmatians, Dacians, Germans, Scythians, and of provinces and islands, many to us unknown and innumerable. (*Against the Jews*)

IMAGES OF THE CHURCH

#6 *In the Old Testament the revelation of the kingdom is often made under the forms of symbols. In similar fashion the inner nature of the Church is now made known to us in various images.*

The Church as Sheepfold

The image of Church as sheepfold vividly commended itself to nomadic peoples in the Middle East and was equally canvassed in the Old Testament ('The Lord is my shepherd',

[22]Text: CCL 2.1354

Ps. 23) and in the New ('I am the good shepherd', Jn. 10). The emphasis is usually more on the shepherd, ever vigilant and caring, than on the sheep. When David killed a bear and a lion without any weapons when they dared attack some of his sheep (1K. 17:28) he gave Caesarius of Arles a prefigure of the devil being confronted by Christ 'in order that his sole Church might be removed from the power or mouth of the devil (hom. 121). Elsewhere (hom. 138) Caesarius links the image of the shepherd with the city seated on a mountain[23]:

> Surely you see a city placed on a mountain. She was found in order to be put on a mountain for she was like the sheep that was lost. Now truly, brethren, who does not see the Catholic Church after she has been revealed? Who found her when she was hidden? As I have said, she is the city, and that one sheep which the shepherd sought when it was lost, and finding it, carried it on his shoulder rejoicing. The shepherd himself is the mountain, the sheep on his shoulder is the city on the mountain... Who does not hear her? Why, she was discovered by Christ and now stands out visible, glorious, admirable, clear, and, to describe her succinctly, universal.

Chromatius of Aquileia (hom. 30) interprets the shepherds guarding their flocks at Christ's birth (Lk.2:8) as the bishops whose role is to secure the safety of the flocks entrusted to them by Christ, a role which always presumes faith in Christ and obedience to His commandments.

The Church as Edifice

This edifice has many names to describe it: the house of God in which his family dwells; the household of God in the Spirit (Eph. 2:19-22), the dwelling place of God among men (Apoc. 21:3); and, especially, the holy temple. This temple, symbolized in places of worship built out of stone, is praised by the Fathers and, not without reason, is compared in the liturgy to the Holy City, the New Jerusalem.

[23] Text: CCL 103.570

Melito of Sardis, in his *On the Pascha*, says:

> 44.[24] The temple here below was once of value, but now it
> is valueless because of Christ above; the earthly Jerusa-
> lem was once of value, but now it is valueless because of
> the heavenly Jerusalem.

The contrast between the old and new Jerusalem was histor-
ically, indeed some of the Fathers thought providentially,
highlighted by the massive destruction of the city in 70 A.D.
The Fathers almost invariably linked the Jewish rejection of
the Messiah to their replacement as the chosen people by the
newly emerged Christian Church.

Melito, in the same context, draws out the consequences
of the cessation of sacrifice in Jerusalem (to which the
celebration of the Paschal sacrifice was restricted by the
Deuteronomic code):

> ...and the model was abolished when the Lord was
> revealed, and today, things once precious have become
> worthless, since the really precious things have been
> revealed.
>
> 44 Once, the slaying of the sheep was precious, but it is
> worthless now because of the life of the Lord; the death of
> the sheep was precious, but it is worthless now because of
> the salvation of the Lord; the blood of the sheep was
> precious, but it is worthless now because of the Spirit of
> the Lord; a speechless lamb was precious, but it is worth-
> less now because of the spotless Son...
>
> 45 The narrow inheritance was precious, but it is
> worthless now because of the widespread grace. For it is
> not in one place nor in a little allotment that the glory of
> God is established, but to all ends of the inhabited earth
> his grace overflows, and there the almighty God has
> pitched his tent through Christ Jesus; to whome be glory
> for ever. Amen.

[24]Text, OECT,22,ed.Hall

The image of the Church as edifice best presents itself with Christ as the corner-stone. Tertullian puts this in its Old Testament perspective in his *Against Marcion*:

> 3.7[25] These tokens of ignobility (cf. Ps. 22:6) apply to the First Coming, as the tokens of sublimity apply to the Second, when he will become no longer a stone of stumbling, or a rock of offence, but the chief corner-stone, taken back again, after rejection, and set on high at the summit of the temple — that is, the Church — that rock, in fact, mentioned by Daniel, which was carved out of a mountain, which will break in pieces and grind to powder the image of the kingdoms of this world. Concerning this Second Coming the same prophet says, "And behold, one like the Son of man coming with the clouds of heaven... and there was given to Him royal power, and all the nations of the earth after their kinds, and all glory to serve, and his power even for ever, that shall not be taken away, and His kingdom that shall not be destroyed" (Dan. 7:13-14).

The Church is not just the material building of God; in Cyprian's illuminating phrase it is 'the House of Faith'.

In his work, *On Mortality* he says:

> 6 [26] God promised immortality and eternity to you leaving this world, and do you doubt? This is not to know God at all... This is, though one is in the Church, not to have faith in the House of Faith.

In a *Homily for Epiphany* Augustine sees Christ as the cornerstone for the union of Jews and Gentiles:

> s.204[27] And it was on that day, which is called his birthday, that the Jewish shepherds saw Him; whereas on this day, which is properly called 'Epiphany', that is 'Manifestation', the Gentile Magi adored Him...Indeed, to both

[25] Text: OECT, tr. E.Evans, 188   [26] Text: CCL 111A.20   [27] Text: PL 38.1037

was He born as a Cornerstone, that as the Apostle says, he might make the two in Himself into one new man, making peace, and might change both to God in the one body by the Cross (Eph. 2:16).

What is a Cornerstone but the joining of two walls coming from different directions, which then, as it were, exchange the kiss of peace? The circumcised and the uncircumcised, that is, the Jews and the Gentiles, obviously were mutual enemies, and that because two radically different things separated them — the worship of the one true God by the Jews, the worship of many false gods by the Gentiles. Since, therefore, the first group were close by, but the other far off, He led both to Himself, He who changed both to God in the one body, by, as the same Apostle adds appropriately, the Cross killing enmities in Himself. And coming, he says, He preached peace to you who were afar off, and peace to those who were near, because through Him we have access both in one spirit to the Father (Eph. 2:11-22).

See if this is not a description of the two walls coming from different directions of enmity, and likewise of the Cornerstone, Jesus the Lord, to whom they have both approached from different directions, in whom they have both agreed, that is, both those of the Jews and those of the Gentiles who have believed in Him.

Clement of Alexandria hails the Church as Mother:

"Their children", Scripture says, "shall be put upon the shoulders, and they shall be comforted held on the knees, as a mother comforts, so will I comfort you" (Isa. 66: 12-13). A mother draws her children close to her. We seek our mother, the Church. (*Paidagogos*, 1.5,21, SC 70.148).

Cyprian, in Epistle 74, has a classic statement on the Church as Mother:

ep.74,5 [28] If he who was born outside the Church can be made a temple of God, why cannot the Holy Spirit also be infused into the temple, for whoever, after his sins have been revealed has been sanctified in baptism and reformed spiritually into a new man has become fit to receive the Holy Spirit since the Apostle says: "As many of you who have been baptized into Christ have put on Christ" (Gal. 3:27). He who, baptized among the heretics, can put on Christ, can much more receive the Holy Spirit whom Christ sent. Otherwise the one sent will be greater than the sender if the one baptized outside should indeed begin to put on Christ, but should not have been able to receive the Holy Spirit, as if either Christ could be put on without the Spirit, or the Spirit separated from Christ. It is also stupid of them to say that although the regeneration, by which we are born in Christ through the washing of a second birth, is spiritual, anyone can be born spiritually among the heretics where they say the Spirit is not. For water alone cannot cleanse sins and sanctify man unless he has the Holy Spirit also.

The Church as Bride of Christ

Methodius of Olympus, in the Third Discourse of his *Symposium*, a work modelled on the dialog of the same name by Plato, but dealing, for the most part, with virginity rather than profane love, in dealing with the image of the Church as the bride of Christ and mother of Christians powerfully develops the image of Christ as Second Adam from whose side the children of the Church are regenerated, like Eve from the side of Adam:

> 3.8 [29] For otherwise the Church could not receive the seed or assure by the bath of regeneration (Tit.3: 5) the rebirth of believers unless for them Christ emptied Himself, as I have said, for their conception of Him in the recapitulation of the Passion, and came down from Heaven to die

[28] Text: CSEL III,2,803   [29] Text: SC 95.108

again, and clung to His bride, the Church, allowing to be removed from His side a power by which all may increase who are founded upon Him, who have been born, thanks to baptism, from His bones and flesh, that is to say, from His holiness and glory. For it is quite correct to say that 'the flesh and bone' of Wisdom is understanding and wisdom, and 'His side' is the 'Spirit of Truth', the Advocate, from whom the illuminated (i.e. the baptized) receive and by whom they are rightly begotten into immortality.

And it is impossible for anyone to participate in the Holy Spirit and to be accounted as a member of Christ unless first the Word has descended upon him and he has fallen into the sleep of ecstasy that, risen from this deep sleep and filled with the Spirit, he may receive rejuvenation and renewal.

Now 'the side' of the Word may truly be called 'the Spirit of Truth', which is septiform according to the prophet; and God, taking from His side during his ecstasy, that is, after His incarnation and passion, prepares a helpmate for Him, that is, all the souls who are betrothed and married to Him. For the Scriptures, in fact, frequently refer in this way to Christ, as the actual multitude and assembly of the faithful taken as a whole, while it is only the perfect who will progress to be the one person and body of the Church, those who are more perfect and have more completely assimilated the truth, those who by their perfect faith and purification from the incongruities of the flesh, become Church and helpmate of Christ. According to the apostle they become the Virgin, espoused and wedded to Him (cf 2 Cor.11:2) and, receiving from Him the fertile seed of doctrine they collaborate in the salvation of others by the help of their proclamation.

As to those who are still imperfect, who have merely begun their lessons in the way of salvation, they are formed and brought to full term by those who are more perfect, by mothers in labor, until they are born and born again into the greatness and beauty of virtue. These too when they make progress become Church and they collaborate in the birth and rearing of other children bringing to full term in the receptive soul, as in a mother's womb, the unaltered will of the Word.

The image of the Church as bride of Christ is also prominent in the early Syriac church. There is a famous hymn in the apocryphal *Acts of Judas Thomas* where the Church is so personified, at least in the Syriac version. In the Greek version (and scholars are in disagreement about which version came first), 'the daughter of light', the subject of the poem, is Sophia, or Wisdom, not the Church:

> [30] My Church is the daughter of light, the splendor of kings is hers. Charming and winsome is her aspect, fair and adorned with every good work. Her garments are like flowers, whose smell is fragrant and sweet. On her head dwells the king, and he feeds his citizens beneath. Truth is placed on her head, joy moves in her feet. Her mouth is open becomingly, and with it she speaks all praises. The twelve apostles of the Son and the Seventy Two resound in her. Her tongue is the curtain which the priest raises to enter. Her neck is the flight of steps which the first Architect built. Her two hands proclaim the life and her ten fingers have opened the gate of heaven.
> Her bridal chamber is lit up and full of the fragrance of salvation. A censer is prepared in its midst, love and faith and hope gladdening all.

Among the Latin Fathers treating of the Church as bride of Christ we give two selections, from Ambrose of Milan and Cyprian of Carthage:
Ambrose, in *On the Christian Faith*, writes:

> 111.72[31] Christ alone, then, is the bridegroom to Whom the Church, His bride, comes from the nations and gives

[30] Trans. R. Murray, *Symbols of Church and Kingdom: A Study in Early Syriac Tradition* , Oxford, Clarendon Press, 1975

[31] Text: PL 16.604-605

herself in wedlock; previously poor and starving, but now rich with Christ's harvest; gathering in the hidden bosom of her mind handfuls of the rich crop and gleanings of the Word, that so she may nourish with fresh food her who is worn out, bereaved by the death of her Son, and starving, she, mother of the dead, but not abandoning the widow and destitute in her search for new children.

73. Christ, then, alone is the bridegroom, begrudging not even the synagogue the sheaves of His harvest. Would that the synagogue had not voluntarily excluded herself!...

74. Who indeed but Christ could dare to claim the Church as His bride, whom He alone, and no other, has called from Libanus, saying: *Come hither from Libanus, my bride, come hither* Or of whom else could the Church have said: *His throat is sweetness, and He is altogether desirable*?...to Whom else but the Word of God could these words apply: *His legs are pillars of marble, set upon bases of gold?*

For Christ alone walks in the souls, and makes His path in the minds of His saints, in which, as upon bases of gold and foundations of precious stone, the heavenly Word has left His footsteps ineffaceably impressed.

75. Clearly we see, then, that both the man and the type are pointing to the mystery of the Incarnation.

Cyprian, in *On the Unity of the Catholic Church*, writes:

6 [32] The bride of Christ cannot be defiled. She is inviolate and chaste. She knows one home only; in all modesty she keeps faithfully to one bridal chamber. It is she who preserves us for God, she who seals for the Kingdom the sons born to her. Whoever breaks with the Church and enters on an adulterous union cuts himself off from the promises made to the Church. He who turns his back on the Church of Christ will not come to the rewards of Christ; he is an alien, a worldling, an enemy. You cannot

[32] Text: OECT, ed. Bévenot, 66

have God for your Father if you no longer have the Church for your mother.

If there was any escape for anyone who was outside the Ark of Noah, there will be the same for one found outside the Church. The Lord warns us when He says: "He that is not with me is against me, and he that gathers not with me scatters" (Mt. 12:30). Whoever breaks the peace and harmony of Christ acts against Christ; whoever gathers elsewhere than in the Church scatters the Church of Christ. The Lord says "I and the Father are one" (Jn. 10:30), and again, it is written of the Father, Son and Holy Spirit, "And the three are one" (1 Jn. 5:8). Does anyone think, then, that this oneness, which derives from God's stability and is welded together after the heavenly pattern can be sundered in the Church and divided by the clash of discordant wills?

Cyril of Jerusalem brings together a number of images for the Church:

> 18.26 [33] Do not be satisfied to ask, 'Where is the church?', but rather, 'Where is the Catholic Church?' For that assuredly is the name of this holy church, the mother of us all. She is the bride of our Lord, Jesus Christ, the only-begotten Son of God (as it is written, 'As Christ also loved the Church and gave Himself for it' (Eph. 5:25). She also presents the image and form of 'Jerusalem which is above', which is free and the mother of us all, once barren but now the mother of many children (cf. Gal. 4:26-27).
>
> For after the rejection of the first church, in the second, the Catholic Church, 'God', as St. Paul says, 'first placed apostles, secondly, prophets, third, teachers, and after that miracles, then gifts of healings, services of help, power of administration, and the speaking of various tongues.' (cf. 1 Cor. 12:28)...
>
> Instructed in this holy, Catholic Church, and conducting ourselves rightly, we shall gain the kingdom of heaven

[33] Text: PG 33.1048

and inherit life everlasting; it is to gain this from the Lord that we endure all things.

The sheet let down from heaven in *Acts* is seen by Caesarius of Arles as an all-encompassing image of the Church (cf. Acts 11:5-10).

> 176.4[34] Perhaps it may be also asked why there was a sheet which contained those animals? This too must have a reason. Now we know that a moth, destructive of other animals, does not attack a sheet. Therefore anybody who wishes to reach the mystery of the Catholic Church should banish from his heart the corruption of evil desires. He should be so utterly confirmed in the faith that he is not riddled with evil thoughts as with moths, if he wishes to arrive at the mystery of that sheet which prefigures the Church.
>
> Why was it let down from Heaven three times, except that all the nations that belong to the four corners of the earth where the Church is spread are baptized in the name of the Trinity? The Church was signified in the four corners which fastened the vessel, for they renew all who believe in the name of the Father, and of the Son, and of the Holy Spirit, in order that they may reach the company and communion of the saints. For this reason the four corners, the four parts of the world, and the triple lowering reveal the mystery of the Trinity. This fact also indicates the number of the twelve apostles, with three each delegated to the four, four times three equals twelve. And since the twelve apostles were destined to preach the mystery of the Trinity in the four corners of the world, for this reason the four corners were let down from Heaven three times.

THE CHURCH, THE BODY OF CHRIST

#7 By communicating his Spirit Christ mystically constitutes as his body those brothers of his who are called

---

[34] Text: CCL 184.715

together from every nation... The head of this body is
Christ... All the members must be formed in his likeness
until Christ be formed in them (cf. Gal. 4:19).

Christ, the one Mediator, established and ceaselessly sus-
tains here on earth His Holy Church, the community of
faith, hope and charity as a visible structure.

Ignatius of Antioch, writing to *the Magnesians*, refers to his
other name *Theophoros*, God-bearer:

> 1 [35] being judged worthy of a most godly name in the
> bonds I bear, I sing of the churches and I pray that in
> them there may be a union of the flesh and spirit of Jesus
> Christ, our life forever; of faith and love, to which
> nothing is preferable, and, most important, of Jesus and
> the Father.

When St. Augustine was asked to write a summary of the
Christian religion he subtitled the resulting work, the *Enchi-*
ridion (Handbook), *On Faith, Hope and Charity:*

> 1.4...for these are the chief, nay rather the only, guiding
> principles of our religion.

And in his *Concerning Baptism Against the Donatists* he
says:

> IV.12,18[36] These are the bonds uniting the members,
> individually and collectively, to the body of Christ. 'In
> good faith, hope and charity one is joined to the unity of
> the Church."

Basil the Great, writing to the bishops of Pontus (ep.203)
says:

> [37] 'For the same Lord who divided the islands from the
> mainland by sea, bound island Christians to mainland

---

[35] Text: SC 10.94   [36] Text: CSEL 51.244
[37] Text: LCL, ed. Deferrari, III.148.

Christians by love. Nothing, brethren, separates us from one another but deliberate estrangement. We have one Lord, one faith, one hope. . . . The hands need each other. The feet steady each other. The eyes possess their clear apprehension from joint agreement.

Through baptism we are formed in the likeness of Christ. Clement of Alexandria has a classic description of baptism in his *Paidagogos*:

> 1.6.26[38]When we are baptized we are enlightened; being enlightened, we become adopted sons; becoming adopted sons, we are made perfect, and becoming perfect, we are made divine.
>
> The very fact that we believe in him and are reborn is perfection of life. For God is by no means powerless. As His will is creation and is called the universe, so his desire is the salvation of men and is called the church.

Methodius, in the *Symposium*, sees one of the chief functions of the Church as mother transforming her subjects into children of God by the sacrament of baptism:

> 8.8 [39] Now I think the Church is here said *to bring forth a man child* (cf. Apoc 12:5) simply because the enlightened spiritually receive the features, and image, and manliness of Christ; the likeness of the Word is stamped upon them and is begotten within them by perfect knowledge and faith, and thus Christ is spiritually begotten in each one. And so it is that the Church is with child and in labor until Christ is formed and born within us, so that each of the saints by sharing in Christ is born again as Christ.
>
> This is the meaning of a passage in Scripture which says: *Touch you not my anointed; and do no evil to my prophets*: (Ps. 104:15); those who are baptized in Christ become, so to speak, other Christs by a communication of the Spirit, and here it is the Church that effects this

---

[38] Text: SC 70.158   [39] Text: SC 95.220;cf.ACW 27.113

transformation into a clear image of the Word. Thus the Word of truth must be stamped and imprinted upon the souls of those who are born again.

For in one Spirit we were all baptized into one body (1 Cor. 12:13).

The great exponent of the unity of the Church among the Fathers was Cyprian. Only the one true Church, he maintains, can have the one true baptism, whatever the heretics think or teach to the contrary.

> Ep.74.4 [40] For if therefore, the Church is not with the heretics because it is one and cannot be divided, and if, therefore, the Holy Spirit is not there because He is one and He cannot be with the profane and the strangers, certainly baptism also, which stands firmly in the same unity, cannot be with the heretics because it can be separated neither from the Church nor from the Holy Spirit.

An even better-known text on unity is found in Cyprian's *On the Unity of the Catholic Church*:

> 7[41] This holy mystery of unity, this unbreakable bond of close-knit harmony is depicted in the Gospel by the seamless garment of our Lord Jesus Christ, which was not divided or cut at all, but when *they drew lots* for Christ's garment to see which of them should put on Christ, it was the undivided garment that was the prize, the garment was won unspoiled and undivided. These are the words of Holy Scripture: *Now as regards His garment, as it was from the upper part woven throughout without a seam, they said to one another: Let us not divide it, but let us cast lots for it, whose it shall be* (Jn. 19:23-24). The 'oneness' with which He was clothed came 'from the upper part', that is, from His Father in Heaven, and could in no way be divided by whoever came to acquire it: it retained its well-knit wholeness indivisibly. That man

[40] Text: CSEL III,2.802   [41] Text: CCL III,1.254

cannot possess the garment of Christ who rends and divides the Church of Christ.

The Unity of the Church Body

As all the members of the human body, though they are many, form one body, so also are the faithful of Christ.

St. John Chrysostom devotes the ninth of his *Homilies on Ephesians* (PG62.69-75) to an exegesis of Eph. 4:1-3, which urges Christians to live up to their calling, and to spare no effort to secure with bonds of peace the unity which the Spirit gives. He asks what that unity is, and says that just as in the body the soul is a unifying principle which makes a unity of all the different members, so the Spirit is given to mankind to unite those of different races and cultures so that old and young, rich and poor, children and youth, men and women, and every soul become, in a manner of speaking, one soul, and more completely so than if they were one body. For the spiritual relationship transcends the natural union of soul and body, the union being more perfect and complete, and the bond preserving it the bond of peace.

Elsewhere (*hom. 1 in 1 Cor.*) Chrysostom summarises this thought like this:

> 1.1[42] The name of the Church is not one of separation but of unity and harmony, and should be one throughout the world, even though churches are scattered in many places.

St. Augustine, in a sermon on Pentecost, says that the Holy Spirit is not available outside the Church, but that by the gift of tongues He was conferred on the Church for unity. This unity he sees symbolised in the number one which has to be added to 'seven times seven' to make up the fifty days between Easter and Pentecost. (s. 268, PL 38. 1231)...

[42] Text: PG 61.13

There is only one Spirit, who, according to His own richness and the needs of the ministries, distributes His different gifts for the welfare of the Church. Among these gifts stands out the grace given to the apostles. To their authority the Spirit Himself subjected even those who were endowed with charisms.

The Fathers like to contrast the unity that prevails in the "great" Church with the dangerously divisive innovations among the heretics, especially the Gnostics.

Irenaeus, in *Against Heresies* writes:

111.12,7 [43] These heretics are proved to be, not disciples of the apostles, but of their own wicked ideas. That is at the bottom of the variety of opinions which flourish among them, in that each one adopted error according to his individual capacity. But the Church throughout the world had a firm foundation in the apostles and persevered in one and the same view with regard to God and His Son.

Tertullian, in his *Prescription of Heretics*:

42.8 [44] The Valentinians have taken the same liberties as Valentinus himself, the Marcionites as Marcion, namely to make innovations in the faith at whim. The heresies, when examined in depth, will be found to be at variance in a good number of details with their founders. Most of them have no churches; they are without mother, without fixed abode, without faith, exiles resembling vagabonds.

The Church as body of Christ is seen in very real genetic terms by Methodius. As a body it can conceive and bring forth Christ's faithful in the sacrament of Baptism. The baptized is seen as taken almost surgically from Christ's body, like Eve being formed from a rib of Adam:

[43] Text: SC 34.228   [44] Text: SC 46.149

3.8[45] the Church could not conceive and bring forth anew
the faithful by *the laver of generation* unless Christ emptied Himself for them too for their conception of Him...in
the recapitulation of His Passion, and came down from
Heaven to die again, and clung to His Spouse the Church,
allowing to be removed from His side a power by which
all may grow strong who are built upon Him, who have
been born by the laver and receive of His flesh and bone,
that is of holiness and glory. Correctly interpreted, the
flesh and bone of Wisdom is understanding and virtue;
and His side is the *Spirit of Truth*, the Advocate, from
whom the illuminated receive and by whom they are
rightly begotten into immortality.

And it is impossible for anyone to participate in the
Holy Spirit and to be counted a member of Christ unless
again the Word has first descended on him and fallen into
the sleep of ecstasy, that he may rise from his own deep
sleep and, filled with the Spirit, receive a renewal and
rejuvenation.

Methodius illustrates this in the person of the apostle, Paul:

3.9[46] When He had not yet become perfect in Christ, he
was first born and nursed: Ananaias preached the Gospel
to him and made a new being of him in Baptism, as is
related in *Acts*. When he had grown to manhood and was
remade and fully developed in spiritual perfection, he was
made into a helpmate and a bride of the Word.

#8 *The visible society and the spiritual community, the
earthly Church and the Church endowed with heavenly
riches, are not to be thought of as two realities...but from
one complex reality... This is the sole Church of Christ
which in the Creed we profess to be one, holy, catholic and
apostolic...*

The radiance of Christ is focused on all men through the
prism of the Church. This animating presence of Christ in

---

[45] Text: SC 95:108; cf. ACW 27.66   [46] Text: SC 95.110

the Church is clearly stated by Origen. In an effort to win converts to Christianity he asserts (in the *Contra Celsum*, 6.48)[47] that the holy Scriptures declare the body of Christ, animated by the Son of God, to be the whole Church of God and the members of this body, considered as a whole, to consist of those who are believers. Just as a soul vivifies a body which does not have of itself the natural power of motion, of a living being, so the Word, arousing and moving the whole body, the Church, to suitable action, awakens each member of the Church so that they do nothing apart from the Word.

Elsewhere in the same work (*Cont. Cels.* 6. 79)[48] he rejects the idea of Celsus that there should everywhere exist many bodies and many spirits like Jesus in order that the whole of humanity might be enlightened by the Word of God. The one Word, he says, was enough, having risen as the Sun of justice, to send forth from Judaea His rays into the souls of all those who were willing to receive Him.

Cyprian, in developing his concept of the unity of the church, insists that the bishops have a primary responsibility to show forth the episcopacy as one and undivided.

> 5 [49] The episcopate is one, the parts of which are held together by the individual bishops. The church is one which with increasing fruitfulness extends far and wide into the multitude just as the rays of the sun are many but the light is one, and the branches of the tree are many but the root is one.... Thus too the Church bathed in the light of the Lord projects its rays over the whole world yet there is one light which is diffused everywhere, and the unity of the body is not dissipated.

A COMMUNITY OF LOVE

In a famous apostrophe to the Church, St. Augustine, in his *The Way of Life of the Catholic Church*, paints a vivid picture of the church as a community of love that reaches out to all:

[47] Text: SC 147.300   [48] Text: SC 147.376   [49] Text: OECT, ed. Bévenot, 64

c.30 [50] For to us Christians this rule of life has been given, that we should love the Lord our God with our whole heart, and our whole soul, and our whole mind and our neighbor as ourself, for "On these two commandments depend the whole Law and the prophets" (Mt. 22, 37). It is with reason, then, O Catholic Church, true mother of Christians, that you command that not only God, in possessing whom we enjoy a life of supreme happiness, should be worshipped in perfect purity and chastity, but you set up no creature for us to adore or be required to serve, and you exclude from that incorruptible and inviolable eternity, to which alone man must subject himself and to which the human soul must cling to escape wretchedness, all that has been made and is subject to time and change...you embrace such love and charity for the neighbor that there is found in you a powerful remedy for the numerous diseases with which souls are afflicted on account of their sins.

You teach and guide children with childlike simplicity, youths with firmness, and the aged with mild persuasion, taking into account their mental age as well as their chronological. You subject women to their husbands in chaste, faithful obedience, not for sexual gratification but for the generation of children and the establishment of domestic society. You set men over their wives, not to make playthings of the weaker sex, but in accordance with the laws of pure, honorable love. You bind children to their parents in a sort of free servitude, and give parents a pious rule over their children. You unite brother to brother in a religious bond stronger and closer than the bond of blood. While preserving the bonds of nature and choice, you unite all those related by kinship or marriage in a bond of mutual love.

You teach servants to cleave to their masters more from the joy of their state than because of the necessity of their condition. You make masters be patient with their servants out of regard for their supreme God who is their

[50] Text: PL 32.1336

common master, making them resort to persuasion rather than force. In recollection of their first parents, you join citizen to citizen, nation to nation, and all men to each other, not merely in society, but in a kind of brotherhood. You teach emperors to look to the welfare of their people, and exhort people to be subject to their emperors. You teach us constantly to whom honor is due, to whom affection, to whom reverence, to whom fear, to whom comfort, to whom admonition, to whom encouragement, to whom instruction, to whom reproof, and to whom punishment, showing us that not all these are due to everyone, but that charity is due to all men and harm to none.

II

The Church, The People of God

SALVATION OF A SINGLE PEOPLE: THE NEW ISRAEL

#9 He has, however, willed to make men holy and have them, not as individuals without any bond or link between them, but rather to make them into a people who might acknowledge him and serve him in holiness. He therefore chose the Israelite race to be his own people and established a covenant with it.

Lumen Gentium devotes an entire chapter to the single image of the Church as the people of God. From the Council debate it can be assumed that this represented something of a setback for those who favored the image of Church as Mystical Body of Christ. For the latter group the People of God image seemed too democratic and too anthropocentric. In reality, of course, it is a profoundly biblical image with deep foundations in both Old and New Testaments and in the Fathers. In the New Testament community the disciples of Jesus saw themselves as the true Israel, as indeed did other Jewish sects — the Pharisees, the Sadducees, the Zealots and the Essenes. Such distinctive features in the Christian community as baptismal initiation, the re-enactment of the Last Supper, the *koinonia* of loving fellowship, the community leadership of the Twelve helped to mark them off from other Jewish religious sects from an early stage, and, after the fall of Jerusalem in 70 A.D. and the expansion of Christianity to the Gentiles, the claim of the Church to be the new Israel and the new people of God became widespread and distinctive.

The Old Testament basis for the image is clearly stated by Clement of Rome in his *Epistle to the Corinthians*:

> 29[1]Let us come before him, then, in sanctity of soul, lifting pure and undefiled hands to him, loving our gentle and merciful Father who has made us his chosen portion. For it is written, "When the Most High divided the nations, when He scattered the sons of Adam, He set up the boundaries of nations according to the number of angels of God. His people Jacob became the portion of the Lord; Israel was the allotment of His inheritance" (Deut. 32:8-9). And in another place it is written, "Behold, the Lord takes to Himself a nation from the midst of nations, as a man takes the first-fruit of his threshing floor, and from that nation shall come forth the Holy of Holies" (Deut. 4:34; 14:2; Numb. 18: 27, Ezech. 48:12).

Melito of Sardis (c. 180 A.D.), in his *Homily on the Pasch*, has a marvellous description of the way in which the Church is the realization of the prefigurations of the Old Testament, the new People of God replacing Israel, the New Law replacing the Old, and the Church taking the place of the temple:

> 39[2] As it is in corruptible images, so it is in incorruptible; as it is in the earthly, so it is in the heavenly. For the Lord's salvation and truth have been prefigured in the people, and the teachings of the Gospel have been proclaimed in the Law. The people were the outline of the plan, and the Law a draft of the parable, but the Gospel is

---

[1]Text: SC 167.146   [2]Text: SC 123. 80-82

the Law explained and fulfilled, and the Church is the receptacle of truth.

41 The model, then, was of value before the reality, and the prefigure was splendid before its fulfillment. That is to say, the people was important before the Church emerged, and the Law was remarkable before the Gospel shed its light. But when the Church was built, and the Gospel preached, the figure was emptied of its meaning, after it had been translated into truth, and the Law was likewise emptied, after it was translated into the Gospel.

Just as the figure becomes redundant when it transmits its image to reality, and the prefigure is made void when it is illuminated by explanation, so also the Law reached its term when the Gospel came to light, and the people went into oblivion when the Church came into existence.

Clement of Alexandria combines in the *Paidagogos* the image of church as mother with the equally powerful one of church as the new people of God:

1.5.19[3] The old people were perverse and hard of heart, but we, the new people, the assembly of little ones, are pliant as a child. In the Epistle to the Romans the Apostle declares that he rejoices in the hearts of the innocent, but notice that he proceeds to circumscribe this childlikeness: "I would have you wise as to what is good, and without guile as to what is evil" (Rom. 16:19)...20. The little ones are indeed the new spirits, who have newly become wise despite their former folly, who have risen up according to the new Covenant. Only recently, in fact, has God become known through the coming of Christ. "For no one has known God but the Son and him to whom the Son has revealed Him" (cf. Mt. 11:27).

Then the New People, in contrast to the Old, are young, because they have heard the new good tidings. The fertile time of life is this unageing youth of ours during which we are always at our intellectual prime, ever young, ever childlike, ever new. For those who have partaken of the New Word must themselves be new. Whatever partakes of eternity *ipso facto* assumes the qualities of the incorruptible. Therefore the name ' childhood' is for us a life-long season of spring, because the truth abiding in us is ageless and our being, made to overflow with that truth, is ageless too. For wisdom is ever fruitful, ever fixed unchangeably on the same truths, ever constant.

For many of the early Fathers the idea of a 'new Israel' was narrowly interpreted as a Christian inheritance to the total exclusion of the Jews. In Melito's *Paschal Homily* there is, among much lyricism and exultant rhapsody at the Resurrection of Christ a painful and embarrassing excoriation of the Jews for their role in the death of Christ. In a forensic setting they are arraigned for murder, leaving Melito with the doubtful honor of being labelled 'the first Christian poet of deicide.' This is a sample of the invective:

> 81[4] O lawless Israel, what is this unprecedented crime you have committed, casting strange sufferings on your Lord and Master, the One who created you, honored you, named you "Israel"? But you have not proved to be "Israel" for you have not seen God; you have not recognized the Lord. You have failed, Israel, to recognize that this is the first-born of God, Who was begotten before the morning star, who made the light to rise and the day resplendent, who separated the darkness and established the first divisions, who fixed the earth in place...who fashioned for Himself man on earth. This was He who chose you for Himself and was your God.

The etymology of 'Israel' was earlier explained by Philo in his treatise, *On the Change of Names*, 81: 'We shall also find that the change of Jacob's name to Israel (cf. Gen. 32:28) is much to the purpose. Why? Because Jacob is the supplanter, and Israel means "he who sees God".

[4] Text: SC 123.106

In Justin's *Dialog with Trypho* the same point is made in greater detail:

> 134[5] If anyone sees a beautiful woman and desires to have her, they quote the experiences of Jacob (called) Israel.... In the marriages of Jacob I shall mention what dispensation and prophecy were accomplished...(cf. Gen.c.29). The marriages of Jacob were types of that which Christ was about to accomplish. For it was not lawful for Jacob to marry two sisters at once.And he serves Laban for one of the daughters, and being deceived in the younger, he again served seven years. Now Leah (the elder) is your people and synagogue, but Rachel is our Church. And for these and for the servants in both, Christ even now serves.... Jacob served Laban for speckled, many-spotted sheep; and Christ served, even to the slavery of the cross, for the various, many-formed races of mankind, acquiring them by the blood and mystery of the Cross. Leah was weak-eyed; for the eyes of your souls are exceedingly weak. Rachel stole the gods of Laban, and has hid them to this day, and we have lost our paternal and material gods. Jacob was hated for all time by his brother, and we now, and our Lord Himself, are hated by you and by all men, though we are brothers by nature. Jacob was called Israel, and Israel has been demonstrated to be the Christ, Who is, and is called Jesus.

Elsewhere in the *Dialog* Justin shows how the Christians become the chosen people, combining texts from Ezechiel, Zachariah and Isaiah:

> 119[6] And after the Just One was put to death, we blossomed forth as another people, and sprang up like new and thriving corn, as the Prophet exclaimed: 'And many nations shall flee unto the Lord in that day for a people; and they shall dwell in the midst of the whole earth' (Zach.2:11). But we Christians are not only a people, but a holy people, as we have already shown: 'And they shall call it a holy people, redeemed by the Lord' (Isa.62:12).

[5]Text: PG 6.785   [6]Text: PG 6.752

Wherefore, we are not a contemptible people, nor a tribe
of barbarians, nor just any nation like the Carian or the
Phrygian, but the chosen people of God.

As in many other subjects Augustine proves himself a mod-
erating influence in insisting that the coming of Christ was
for the salvation of Jew and Gentile alike. He makes the
point very strikingly in a Homily on the Epiphany by
emphasizing that the Jewish shepherds saw the new-born
Christ on the Nativity and the Gentile Magi adored Him on
the feast of Epiphany a few days later, angels announcing
Him to the former, stars to the latter. But since the heavens
are inhabited by the angels and are adorned by the stars, to
both did the heavens show forth the glory of God:

> 204.2[7] Indeed to both was He born as a cornerstone, that,
> as the Apostle says, "He might make the two in Himself
> into one new man, making peace, and might change both
> to God into the one body by the Cross"(Eph. 2:15).
>
> What is a corner but the joining of two walls coming
> from different directions, which then, so to speak,
> exchange the kiss of peace? The circumcised and the
> uncircumcised, that is the Jews and the Gentiles,
> obviously were mutual enemies; and that because two
> radically different things separated them — the worship
> of the one true God by the former, the worship of many
> false gods by the latter. Since, therefore, the one group
> was near at hand but the other far off, He led both to
> Himself, "He who changed both to God in the one body,
> by", as the same apostle adds appropriately, "the Cross
> killing enmities in Himself. And coming", he says "He
> preached peace to you that were afar off and peace to
> those who were near, because through Him we have
> access both in one spirit to the Father" (Eph. 2:16, 17).

St. Cyril of Jerusalem passes in review some of the main
historical phases in the history of Israel as God's original
choice as his chosen people:

[7]Text: PL 38.1037

XVIII.24[8] Aptly is the Church named *Ecclesia*, i.e. assembly, because it calls forth and assembles all men, as the Lord says in Leviticus: *Then assemble the whole community at the entrance of the Meeting Tent* (Lev.8:3). It is worth noting that this word 'assemble' is used in the Scriptures for the first time in the passage when the Lord assembled Aaron in the high priesthood. In Deuteronomy God says to Moses: *Assemble the people for me; I will have them hear my words, that they may learn to fear me* (Deut.4:10). He mentions the name of the Church again when He says of the tablets: *And on them were inscribed all the words that the Lord spoke to you on the mountain from the midst of the fire on the day of the assembly* (Deut. 9:10), as if He would say more plainly "on the day on which you were chosen and became a Church".

Cyril goes on to explain how the New Covenant succeeded the Old, the New People of God replacing the chosen 'Israel':

18.25[9] The Psalmist of old had sung: *In the Church bless God; bless the Lord God, you of Israel's wellspring* (Ps.6:27). But when the *Jews for their plots against the Saviour were cast down from* grace, the Saviour established from the Gentiles a second holy Church, the Church of us Christians, concerning which He said to Peter: *And upon this rock I will build my Church, and the gates of Hell shall not prevail against it* (Matt.16:18).

Prophesying plainly of both these churches David said of the first, which was rejected: *I hate the assembly of the evildoers* (Ps.25:5), and of the second, which is built up, he says in the same Psalm: *O Lord, I have loved the beauty of thy house* (Ps. 25:8), and immediately afterwards, *In the assemblies I will bless thee, O Lord* (Ps.25:12). For after the rejection of the first Church in Judea, the Churches of Christ are multiplied throughout the world.

[8]Text: PG 33.1044   [9]Text: PG 33.1045

When Origen is explaining the first commandment of the Decalog in his *Homilies on Exodus* he shows how Christianity inherited the special status originally intended for Israel:

VII.12[10] Scripture itself will be able to teach us the reason for "many gods" or "many lords"... For the same Moses says in the song of Deuteronomy, "When the Most High divided the nations and scattered the sons of Adam, he set the boundaries of the nations in accordance with the number of the angels of God. And his people Jacob became the portion of the Lord, the lot of his inheritance, Israel." (Deut. 32:8-9)

You, therefore, O people of Israel, who are "the portion of God" who were made "the lot of His inheritance", "shall not have" it says, "other gods besides me" (Ex. 20:3) because God is truly "one God" and the Lord is truly "one Lord."

But do not think that these words are spoken only to that "Israel" which is "according to the flesh" (cf. 1 Cor. 10:18). These words are addressed much more to you who were made Israel spiritually by living for God, who were circumcised, not in the flesh, but in heart. For although we are Gentiles in the flesh, we are Israel in spirit because of Him who said, "Ask of me and I will give you the Gentiles as your inheritance and the ends of the earth as your possession" (Ps. 2:8), and because of Him who also said," Father, all things that are mine are thine, and thine are mine, and I am glorified in them (Jn. 17:10), if only you so act that you may be worthy to be "a portion" of God and to walk in "the lot of his inheritance." And those who formerly were brought out of "the house of bondage", now again — "because he who sins is a slave of sin" (Jn. 8:34) are slaves no longer to the Egyptians alone, but to all nations. Therefore, to you also who went out of Egypt through Jesus Christ and were brought "out of the house of bondage", it is said "You shall not have other gods besides me" (Ex. 20:3).

[10]Text: PG 12.352; cf. FOTC 71.319-320 tr. R.E.Heine

A PRIESTLY PEOPLE

#10 *Eusebius of Caesarea, in his* Ecclesiastical History *(1.3) has a clear statement of Christ's triple messianic role of priest, prophet and king:*

1.3.7[11] And not only those who were honored with the high priesthood, and who, for the sake of the symbol were anointed with specially prepared oil, were adorned with the name of Christ among the Hebrews, but also the kings whom the prophets anointed under the influence of the Divine Spirit, and thus constituted, so to speak, typical Christs. For they also bore in their persons types of the royal and sovereign power of the true and only Christ, the Divine Word, who rules over all. And we have been told further that certain of the prophets themselves became, by the act of anointing, Christs in prototype, so that all these prefigure the true Christ, the divinely inspired and heavenly Word, who is the only high priest of all, and the only King of every creature, and the Father's only supreme prophet of prophets.

And a proof of this is that no one of those of old who were symbolically anointed, whether priests, or kings, or prophets, possessed so great a power of inspired virtue as was shown by our Lord and Savior Jesus, the true and only Christ. None of them, at any rate, however superior in dignity and honor they may have been for many generations among their own people, ever gave the name of 'Christians' to their followers from the name 'Christ' which they had in prototype. Neither did their subjects ever bestow divine honor on any of them; nor after their death were their followers disposed to die for the one whom they had honored.

And never did so much excitement arise among all the nations of the earth in regard to any one of that age; for the mere prototype could not act with such power among them as the realization of that type, exhibited by our

[11]Text: SC 31.14

Savior. Although He had received no symbols and types of high priesthood from any one, although He had not been born of a race of priests, although He was not elevated to a kingdom by military guards, although He was not a prophet like those of old, He was nevertheless adorned by the Father with all three, if not with the symbols, yet with the truth itself. And so, although He did not possess similar honors to those already mentioned, He, more than any of them, is called Christ. And as the true and only Christ of God, He has filled the whole earth with the truly august and sacred name of Christians, committing to His followers no longer types and images, but the revealed virtues themselves, and a heavenly life in the very doctrines of truth.

St. John Chrysostom has a similar reflection on the triple function of priest, prophet and king in *Homily 3 on the Second Epistle to the Corinthians:*

> 3.5[12] And that which is 'anointed' and 'sealed' gave the Spirit by which He did both these things, making at the same time prophets, priests, and kings, for in olden times these three types were anointed. But now we have not just one but all three of these dignities preeminently. For we are the first to enjoy a kingdom, and secondly, we are made priests by offering our body for a sacrifice (Rom. 12:1), and thirdly, we are constituted prophets, for 'what eye has not seen, nor ear heard '(1 Cor. 2:9) has been revealed to us.

Fastidius, a bishop in early Christian Britain, begins his work *On the Christian Life*[13] with a consideration of the nomenclature 'Christian':

> None of the wise and faithful is unaware of the fact that Christ signifies 'anointed'. It is obvious that none except

---

[12]Text: PG 61.411   [13]Text: PL 50.384

holy men, worthy of God, were anointed, and none other except prophets, priests, and kings. And so great was the mystery of this anointing that, far from it being general among the Jewish people, very few of the majority deserved to receive it. This was so until the coming of our Lord Jesus Christ whom God anointed with the oil of gladness, that is with the Holy Spirit, *myrrh and aloes waft from your robes* (Ps. 45:8). From that time those believers who have been cleansed by the sanctification of baptism, not few as was formerly under the Law, but all, are anointed as prophets, priests, and kings.

St. Ambrose in his work *On the Sacraments* connects the priesthood of the laity to baptism:

4.1[14] In the Old Testament the priests were accustomed to enter the outer temple frequently; the chief high priest entered the inner temple once a year. The Apostle Paul, obviously recalling this to the Hebrews, explains the sequence of the Old Testament, for the manna was in the inner tabernacle, and also the rod of Aaron, that had withered and afterwards blossomed, and the censer.

What is the significance of this? So that you may understand what the inner sanctuary is, into which the priest led you, into which the chief high priest is accustomed to enter once a year, namely; the baptistery, where the rod of Aaron flourished. Formerly, it was dry; afterwards it blossomed: 'And you were dried, and you begin to flower by the watering of the font' (cf. Virgil, *Georgics* 4.32). You had become dry by sins, you had become dry by errors and transgressions, but now you began to bring forth fruit 'planted near the running waters' (Ps. 1:3).

But perhaps you may say: What was this to the people if the rod of the priest had become dry and blossomed again? What is the people itself, if not of the priest? To these it was said: 'But you are a chosen generation, a royal priesthood, a holy nation', as the Apostle Peter says (1

[14] Text: CSEL 73.46

Pet. 2:9). Everyone is anointed into the priesthood, is anointed into the Kingdom, but the spiritual kingdom is also the spiritual priesthood.

THE SACRAMENTS AS MEANS OF SALVATION

#11. *The sacred nature and organic structure of the priestly community is brought into operation through the sacraments and the exercise of the virtues.*

Baptism as Rite of Initiation

Incorporated into the Church through baptism, the faithful are appointed by their baptismal character to their Christian religious worship....

The rite of initiation and its consequences are clearly described in the *First Apology* of Justin Martyr:

> 61[15] We will not fail to explain how we consecrated ourselves to God when we received regeneration through Christ. Those who are convinced and believe what we say and teach is true, and pledge that they will be able to live accordingly, are taught by prayer and fasting to ask God to forgive their past sins, while we pray and fast with them. Then we lead them to a place where there is water, and they are regenerated in the same way in which we ourselves were regenerated. In the name of God the Father and Lord of all, and in the name of our Saviour, Jesus Christ, and of the Holy Spirit they then receive the washing with water. For Christ said: 'Unless you be born again, you shall not enter into the kingdom of heaven'. 65 After baptizing in this manner the one who has believed, and given his assent, we escort him to the place where are assembled those whom we call brethren, to offer up sincere prayers in common for ourselves, for the baptized person, and for all other persons wherever they be, so that, since we have found the truth, we may be

[15] Text: PG 6.420

considered fit through our deeds to be esteemed as good citizens and observers of the law, and thus attain eternal salvation.

Origen is keenly aware of the social dimensions of the sacraments: 'a single sinner tarnishes the people' (Hom. VII.6 on Joshua, PG 12. 861), and 'one who commits fornication, or another crime, casts a stain on the whole people'.[16]

Cyprian, in Letter 74[17], insists on connecting baptism and church membership:

> 6. But what of the assertion and contention that they who have not been born in the Church can be the sons of God? For the blessed Apostle makes manifest and proves that it is baptism in which the old man dies and the new man is born, saying: "He saved us through the bath of regeneration" (Tit. 3:5). But if regeneration is in the bath, that is in baptism, how can a heresy, which is not the spouse of Christ, generate sons to God through Christ? For it is the Church alone which, joined and united to Christ, spiritually generates sons, according to the same Apostle again saying: "Christ loved the Church and delivered Himself up for her, that He might sanctify her, cleansing her in the bath of water" (Eph. 5: 25-26). If this, therefore, is the beloved and the Spouse, who alone is sanctified by Christ, and alone is cleansed by His bath, it is clear that heresy, which is not the spouse of Christ, can neither be cleansed nor sanctified by His bath, and cannot generate sons to God.

Confirmation and Eucharist

St. Ambrose, in his work *The Mysteries*, shows us the central place occupied by the Eucharist in the Church of Milan. He links Baptism, Confirmation and Eucharist in his exposition of the rites of initiation:

[16]Text: PG 12.244; cf. FOTC 71.210, tr. R.E.Heine   [17]Text: CSEL 111,2.804

7.42[18] Recall, therefore, that you have received a spiritual seal, "the spirit of wisdom and of understanding, the spirit of counsel and fortitude, the spirit of knowledge and of piety, the spirit of holy fear" (Isa. 11:2-3), and preserve what you have received. God the Father sealed you. Christ the Lord confirmed you and gave you a pledge, the Spirit, in your hearts, as you have learned in the reading of the Apostle (cf. 11 Cor. 1:21,22).

8.43 The cleansed people, rich in these insignia, hasten to the altars of Christ, saying: 'And I shall go unto the altar of God Who gives joy to my youth' (Ps. 42:4). . . . Thou hast prepared a table in my sight. . . .

8.47 It has been proved that the sacraments of the Church are more ancient; now realize that they are more powerful. In fact it is a marvellous thing that God rained manna on the fathers, and that they were fed by daily nourishment from heaven. Therefore, it is said 'Man has eaten the bread of angels' (Ps. 77:25). Yet all those who ate that bread died in the desert but this food which you receive, this 'living bread, which came down from heaven,' furnishes the substance of eternal life, and whoever eats this bread 'will not die forever'; for it is the body of Christ.

St. Ambrose, in his work *On the Sacraments*, emphasises that the Eucharist should become our daily bread:

5.25[19] If bread is 'daily', why do you take it after a year as the Greeks in the East are accustomed to do? Receive daily what is of benefit to you daily. So live that you may deserve to receive it daily. He who does not deserve to receive it daily does not deserve to receive it annually ... Then do you hear that, as often as the sacrifice is offered, the death of the Lord, the resurrection of the Lord, the ascension of the Lord, is signified, and the remission of sins, and do you not take this bread of life daily? He who has a wound requires medicine. The fact that we are under sin is a wound: the medicine is the heavenly and venerable sacrament.

[18] Text:CSEL 73.106,109   [19] Text: CSEL 73.69

St. Cyprian, in his commentary *On the Lord's Prayer*, links the Eucharist as principle of salvation and abiding token of membership of the Church:

> 18[20]... Now we request that this bread be given to us daily lest we, who are in Christ, and who daily receive His Eucharist for food for salvation, should by the interposition of some heinous crime, be witheld from communion and forbidden the heavenly food, and so be separated from the Body of Christ.... Consequently, we pray that 'our Bread', that is, Christ, may be given to us 'daily', so that we who abide and live in Christ may not fall away from His sanctification and His Body.

Sacrament of Reconciliation

St. Augustine, in his *Enchiridion*, notes that belief in the forgiveness of sins is expressed in the Creed immediately after belief in the holy Church:

> 64.17[21] Therefore, in the order of the Creed, after the reference to "holy Church" comes reference to "forgiveness of sins." For it is by this that the role of the Church on earth stands; it is by this that 'what was lost and is found again' (Lk. 15:24) is not lost again. Now the gift of baptism is, of course, an exception. It is an antidote given to us against original sin, so that what is contracted by being born is removed by being born again, though it also takes away actual sins as well, whether of heart, word or deed. But, apart from this great remission — the beginning point of man's renewal, in which all guilt, original and actual is washed away — the rest of life, after reaching the use of reason, no matter how resolutely we progress in virtue is not without the need for the forgiveness of sins. This is so because the sons of God, as long as they live this mortal life, are in a conflict with death. And, although it is truly said of them, "As many as are led by the Spirit of God, they are the sons of God" (Rom. 8:14),

---

[20] Text: CCL 111A.101   [21] Text: PL40.262

yet even as they are led by the Spirit of God and, as sons of God, advance toward God, they are also being led by their own spirits, so that, burdened by the corruptible body and under the influence of certain human feelings, they thus fall away and commit sin. But it is a matter of proportion. Although every crime is a sin, not every sin is a crime. Thus, we can say of the life of holy men, even while they exist in this mortal state, that they are found without crime. "But if we say that we have no sin", as the great apostle says, "we deceive ourselves, and the truth is not in us." (1 Jn.1:8)

65 Nevertheless, no matter how great our crimes, forgiveness for them should never be despaired of in holy church by those who truly repent, each in proportion to his sin. And, in the act of repentance, when a crime has been committed of such gravity as also to lead to exclusion of the sinner from the body of Christ, we should consider not so much the measure of time as the measure of sorrow. For, "a contrite and humbled heart God will not despise" (Ps. 51:17).

Still, since the sorrow of one heart is generally concealed from another, and does not become obvious through words and similar signs — even when it is obvious to Him of whom it is said, "My groaning is not concealed from you" (Ps. 38:9) — times of repentance have been rightly established by those placed over the churches, that satisfaction may also be made in the Church, in which the sins are forgiven. For, of course, outside her the sins are not forgiven. For she alone has received the pledge of the Holy Spirit (2 Cor.1:22) without whom there is no forgiveness of sins. Those forgiven thus obtain life everlasting.

This text illustrates the fact that Penance has not just a personal but has also an ecclesial dimension.

Marriage and the Christian Family

Pope Paul VI explains the expression' the family, the

domestic Church' in his exhortation, *Evangelii nuntiandi*:
'this signifies that in each Christian family different aspects
of the whole church are to be found'. The concept 'domestic
church' is found in John Chrysostom, in *Homily XX on the
Epistle to the Ephesians*:

> 20[22] "A man shall leave his father and mother" (Eph.
> 5:31). But he does not add "and shall dwell with", but
> "shall cleave to", thus showing the closeness of the union
> and the fervent love. Indeed, he is not content with this,
> but by his further remarks he explains the commitment in
> such a way that the two no longer appear as two. He does
> not say "one spirit", he does not say "one soul", for that is
> self-evident and within anyone's capacity, but he says "so
> as to be one flesh." The wife is a second authority, having
> real authority and a considerable equality of dignity, but
> at the same time the husband has somewhat more authority. That is the basis for the well-being of the household.
>
> For he took that former argument, the example of
> Christ, to show that we ought not merely love, but also
> govern, "that she may be", it says, "holy and without
> blemish" (Eph. 5:27). But the word 'flesh' has reference to
> love — and the word 'shall cleave' has likewise reference
> to love. But if you make her 'holy and without blemish'
> everything else will follow. Seek the things which are of
> God, and those which are of man will easily follow.
> Govern your wife and the whole house will be in harmony
> accordingly. Hear what Paul says, "And if they wish to
> learn anything, let them ask their husbands at home" (1
> Cor. 14:35). If we thus regulate our own homes, we shall
> also be ready for the management of the Church. For
> indeed, a home is a church in miniature. So, by becoming
> good husbands and wives, we can surpass all others.

He goes on to find in the Book of Genesis role models of
family life by which the harmony of the Church can be
reproduced in embryo:

[22] Text: PG 62.142

Consider Abraham, and Sarah, and Isaac, and the three hundred and eighteen born in his house (cf. Gen. 14:14). How the whole house was harmoniously knit together, how it was filled with piety, and fulfilled the injunction of the Apostle. She also reverenced her husband, for hear her words: It has not yet happened to me until now and my husband is old also (Gen. 18:12). And the young child was virtuous and the slaves born in the house were excellent too.

Ambrose of Milan says: "Let a husband guide his wife like a pilot, honor her like a partner for life, and share with her as a joint heir of grace" (ep. 63). His even-handed attitude to women is also apparent in his work, *On Widows* 3.16 "All have an example to imitate virgins, married women and widows. Perhaps, therefore, the Church is a virgin, a married woman, and a widow because they are all one body in Christ."

SENSUS FIDELIUM

#12 *By this appreciation of the faith, aroused and sustained by the Spirit of truth, the People of God, guided by the sacred teaching authority (magisterium), and obeying it, receives not the mere word of men, but truly the word of God....*

Tertullian, in his *Prescription against Heretics*, raises the intriguing possibility that, granted that the apostles transmitted the whole doctrine of truth, might the churches have been unfaithful in handing it on?

> c.28 [23]Grant then, that all have erred, that the apostle was mistaken in giving His testimony, that the Holy Spirit was not so attached to any one church as to lead it into truth, although that was why He was sent by Christ, having petitioned the Father that He might be the teacher of truth (cf. Jn. 15:26); grant that He also, the steward of

[23]Text: SC46.124

God, the vicar of Christ, neglected His office, permitting
the churches for a time to have different understandings
and different beliefs concerning what He Himself was
preaching through the apostles — is it likely that so many
and so great churches should have wandered erratically
into one and the same faith? Casual distribution among
the many does not terminate in a single, self-same prod-
uct. Error of doctrine among the churches of necessity
would have produced a variety of products. When, however, what was deposited among many is found to be one
and the same, it is not the consequence of error but of
tradition. How can anyone then, be so reckless as to say
that those who handed on the tradition were in error.

This infallibility of believing Christians, this *sensus fide-
lium*, which extends in Augustine's phrase,' from the
bishops down to the last member of the laity' (PL 44.980)
guarantees, thanks to the Spirit of Truth, that the People of
God cannot err in its prophetic role in matters of faith and
morals.

Origen argues that the churches are so much better than
their secular counterparts, the political assemblies. He
writes in *Against Celsus:*

> 3.29[24] The God who sent Jesus... made the Gospel of
> Jesus to prevail throughout the entire world for the con-
> version and reformation of men, and caused churches
> everywhere to be established to counteract those of
> superstitious, licentious and wicked men; for such is the
> character of the multitude of those who constitute the
> citizens in the assemblies of the various cities. Whereas
> the Churches of God which are instructed by Christ,
> when carefully distinguished from the assemblies in the
> districts in which they are assembled, are as beacons in
> the world; for who would not admit that even the inferior
> members of the Church, and those who in comparison
> with the better are less worthy, are nevertheless more

[24] Text: SC 136.70

excellent than many of those who belong to the (secular) assemblies in those cities.

c.30 For the Church of God, for instance at Athens, is a meek and stable body, one which desires to please God, who is over all things, whereas the assembly of the Athenians is given to sedition, and is in no way comparable to the Church of God in that city.

And you may say the same thing of the Church of God at Corinth, and of the popular assembly at Corinth, and also of the Church of God at Alexandria and the popular assembly of Alexandria. And if the one who hears this is candid and a seeker after truth in his investigations he will be filled with admiration for Him who not only conceived the design but also was also able to ensure everywhere the establishment of Churches of God alongside of the popular assemblies in each city.

Similarly, if one compared the council of the Church of God with the city council anywhere, one would find that certain Church council members are worthy to rule in the city of God if there be any such city in the whole world, whereas the councillors in any other place reveal in their characters no quality worthy of the conventional superiority which they seem to enjoy over their fellow citizens.

CHRIST, TEACHER, KING AND PRIEST OF ALL

#13 This People, therefore whilst remaining one and only one, is to be spread throughout the whole world. . . God sent his son. . . that he might be teacher, king and priest of all. . .

For Justin Martyr, in his *Dialog with Trypho*, Christ is King of Israel, and Christians are the true race of Israel:

> 135[25] And when Scripture says: 'I am the Lord God, the Holy one of Israel, who have made known Israel, your King (Isa. 43:15), will you not understand that Christ is truly the everlasting King? For you understand that

[25] Text: PG 6.788

Jacob, the son of Isaac, was never a king.... Is it Jacob the patriarch in whom the Gentiles and yourselves will trust? Or is it not rather Christ? As, therefore, Christ is the Israel and the Jacob, even so we, who have been quarried out from the bowels of Christ, are the true race of Israel. But let us pay attention to the very words of Scripture: 'I will create a race from Jacob, and heirs to my mountains from Judah. My chosen shall inherit them, my servants live in them. Sharon will be a pasture for flocks, the valley of Achor a feeding place for oxen for the people who have sought me. But you who have abandoned Yahweh, and have forgotten my holy mountain, and prepared a table for demons, and filled out a drink for the demon, I shall give you to the sword. You shall all fall to slaughter, for I called you and you answered not. You did evil before me, and chose what I was displeased at' (Isa. 65: 9-12) Such are the words of Scripture. Understand therefore, that the seed of Jacob now referred to is something else, and does not refer to your people as you suppose.

Clement of Alexandria testifies to the kingly nature of the Christian in his *Stromata*, using a text from Plato's *Statesman* to support his position:

11.18[26] Just as the science of a true king is kingly science and the one who possesses it, whether he is a ruler or a private individual, is rightly called kingly because of his skill (Plato, *Stat*.259AB) so those who have believed in Christ are, and are called good, just as those are really kingly who are concerned with the king. For just as 'the wise are wise thanks to wisdom, and the law-abiding are law-abiding thanks to law, so Christians, disciples of Christ, are kingly thanks to Christ the King.

In a poem at the end of the *Paidagogos*[27] Clement has a similar thought:

[26]GCS 2.122   [27]GCS 1.291

O thou King of saints, Word of the Father on high,
Thou Governor of all things, Ruling ever wisely,
Balm for all labors, Fount of endless joy,
Jesus, holy Saviour of men who cry to thee...
O all-hallowed Shepherd, Guide us, thy children,
Guide thy sheep safely, O King.

In a fragment of Clement of Alexandria, commenting on the parable of the mustard seed, (Mt. 13-32) we read[28]:

To such increased size did the growth of the Word come, that the tree which sprung from it (that is the Church of Christ, established over the whole earth) filled the world so that the fowls of the air, that is, divine angels and lofty souls, dwelt in its branches.

Saint Peter Chrysologus, in a sermon on the same parable, says:

s.98[29] Christ as man received the grain of mustard seed, that is, Christ as man received that kingdom of God which He as God had always possessed. He cast the seed into His garden, that is, into His spouse, the Church. He is often mindful of this garden in the Canticle of Canticles, when he speaks of 'a garden enclosed.' The Church is the garden, spread through her worship over all the world by the plough of the Gospel. She is a garden enclosed by the goads of her discipline, and cleared of all weeds by the labor of the Apostles. She is a garden beautiful to see because of the young trees of the faithful, the lilies of the virgins, the roses of the martyrs, the verdure of the confessors. She is fragrant with unfailing flowers.

Accordingly, Christ cast this grain of mustard seed into His garden, that is, because of the promise of His kingdom. The seed had its roots in the Patriarchs, and grew in the Apostles. In the Church it became a great tree, and through the gifts it produced numerous branches which

---

[28] Text: GCS 3.226   [29] Text: PL 52.476

the Apostle enumerates when He says: 'To one is given the utterance of wisdom; to another the utterance of knowledge, to another the gift of healing, to another the working of miracles; to another prophecy, to another the distinguishing of spirits; to another various forms of tongues' (1 Cor. 12; 8-10).

This character of universality which adorns the People of God is a gift from the Lord himself whereby the Catholic ceaselessly and efficaciously seeks for the return of all humanity...under Christ the head in the unity of His Spirit.

Irenaeus sees Christ summing up, recapitulating, all things in Himself:

111.16,6[30] ...as in super-celestial, spiritual and visible things the Word of God is supreme, so also in things visible and corporeal, He might possess the supremacy and, taking to Himself the pre-eminence, as well as constituting Himself Head of the Church. He might draw all things to Himself at the proper time.

St. Cyril of Jerusalem summarises the reasons why the Church is called 'catholic':

18.23[31] This Church is called Catholic because it is spread throughout the world from end to end of the earth; also because it teaches universally and completely all the doctrines which men should know concerning things visible and invisible, heavenly and earthly; and because it subjects to right worship all mankind, rulers and ruled, lettered and unlettered; further because it treats and heals universally all sorts of sin committed by soul and body; and it possesses in itself every conceivable virtue, whether in deeds, words, or in spiritual gifts of every kind.

Furthermore Cyril testifies to the spread of the Catholic Church throughout the known world:

[30] Text: SC 34.292   [31] Text: PG 33.1044

18.27[32]By the armor of righteousness on the right hand and on the left whether honored or dishonored (cf. 2 Cor.6:7-8) this Church, in days of old, when persecutions and afflictions abounded, wove chaplets for the holy martyrs from the many tints and flowers of patience. And now, when God has favored us with times of peace, this Church receives from emperors and men of high rank, as from men of every condition and race, the honor that is due her. And while the leaders of the nations in this or that part of the earth have borders set to their dominion, the holy Catholic Church alone bears sway in all the world, and knows no boundaries, as it is written: *for God hath made her border peace* (Ps. 147:14).

Cyril of Jerusalem, also in *Catechesis XVIII*, bears eloquent testimony to the fact that 'all men are called to belong to the new People of God'.

18.22[33]The Creed which we repeat contains in sequence, "and in one baptism of repentance unto the remission of sins; and in one, holy catholic church, and in the resurrection of the flesh, and in life everlasting."

Let me complete what remains to be said concerning the article, "And in one, holy, catholic church", concerning which there is much to be said, but our treatment will be brief.

23 The church is called catholic because it is spread throughout the world, from end to end of the earth; also because it teaches universally and completely all the doctrines men need to know concerning things visible and invisible, heavenly and earthly; and because it requires right worship of all mankind, rulers and ruled, literate and illiterate; further because it treats and heals universally every kind of sin committed by soul or body, and it possesses in itself every conceivable virtue, whether in deeds, words, or in spiritual gifts of every kind.

---

[32]Text: PG 33.1048; cf.FOTC 64.135   [33]Text: PG 33.1044

Optatus, Bishop of Milevis, in Numidia, North Africa, wrote a treatise in six books in 365 against the Donatist bishop, Parmenian, head of a fanatical sect later opposed by Augustine, which claimed that it alone was the true church. In an eloquent section of his rebuttal Optatus defines the word 'catholic':

> 2.1[34] You, my brother Parmenian, have said that (the church) is with you alone. This, I presume, is because, in your pride, you are eager to claim some special holiness for yourselves, so that the Church may be where you please, and not where you do not want it. And so, in order that she may be with you in a small corner of Africa, one corner in one small region, is she not to be with us in another part of Africa? Is she not to be in Spain, in Gaul, in Italy, where you are not? If you insist that she is with you only, is she not to be in Pannonia, in Dacia, Moesia, Thrace, Achaia, Macedonia and all of Greece, where you are not? To enable you to argue that she is with you, she is banished from Pontus, Galatia, Cappadocia, Pamphylia, Phrygia, Cilicia, the three Syrias, the two Armenias, all of Egypt and Mesopotamia where you are not. And is she not to be in countless islands and innumerable provinces where you are not? Where in that case shall be the application of the Catholic name, since the Church is called Catholic precisely because she is in accordance with reason and is scattered all over the world? For if you limit the Church just as you please into a narrow corner, if you withdraw whole peoples from her communion, where will that be which the Son of God has merited, where will that be which the Father has freely granted to Him, saying: "I will give to thee the nations for thine inheritance, and the ends of the earth for Thy possession" (Ps. 2:8).

THE CHURCH, NECESSARY FOR SALVATION

#14 *The Church, a pilgrim now on earth, is necessary for salvation.*

[34]Text: CSEL 26.32

The laconic *extra ecclesiam nulla salus* (outside the church there is no salvation) has occasioned much grief and controversy down the ages. One of the earliest statements of the view, a text that is seldom quoted, occurs in an anonymous Paschal homily in the tradition of Origen.[35]

> The victim is eaten in its entirety in a single house, and no flesh is taken outside. This means that only one house has salvation in Christ, namely, the Church throughout the world, hitherto estranged from God but now enjoying unique intimacy with God because it has received the apostles of the Lord Jesus, just as of old the house of Rahab, the harlot, received the spies of Joshua, and was the only one saved in the destruction of Jericho.
>
> So, however numerous the Hebrew houses were, they were equivalent to a single house, and likewise the churches throughout town and country, however numerous they are, constitute but a single Church. For Christ is one in all of them everywhere, Christ who is perfect and indivisible. Therefore in each house the victim was perfect and was not divided among different houses. For Paul himself says that "we are all one in Christ because there is one Lord and one faith" (Eph. 4:5).

Cyprian of Carthage is discussing the same text in *Exodus* in his better-known formulation of the same view in his *Unity of the Church*:

> 8[36] God speaks, saying: "In one house it shall be eaten, you shall not carry the flesh outside of the house". The flesh of the Christ and the holy body of the Lord cannot be carried outside, and there is no other house for believers except the one Church. This house, this hospice of unanimity the Holy Spirit designates and proclaims when He says: God Who makes those of one mind to dwell in His house (Ps. 67:6). In the house of God, in the Church of Christ, those of one mind dwell; they persevere there in concord and simplicity.

[35]Text: SC 36.65, ed. Nautin.   [36]Text: OECT,ed., Bévenot, 70

The mode of entry into this house is baptism, as is clear from the following passage from St. Augustine's *The Trinity:*

> XV.19.34[37] This is the house which, as the Psalm sings, (Ps.1) is built after the captivity, since the house of Christ, called the Church, is built of those rescued from the devil who had held them captive.... And that the devil might not draw into eternal perdition with himself those who would one day be members of His sacred Head, Christ bound him first by the chains of justice, and then by those of power. Hence the devil himself has been called the captivity which He, who ascended to Heaven led captive, and gave gifts to men, or received them in men.
>
> (35) But when the Apostle Peter spoke to the Jews of Christ, as we read in that canonical book in which the Acts of the Apostles are recorded, their hearts were moved; they said to him: 'Brethren, what should we do? Show us.' He said to them, 'Do penance, and let every one of you be baptized in the name of the Lord Jesus Christ, for the forgiveness of sins and you shall receive the gift of the Holy Spirit.' (cf. Acts 2:37-38).

In the *Enchiridion,* when he is examining the articles of the Creed sequentially, Augustine shows the connections between 'I believe in the Son' and 'I believe in the Holy Spirit' and 'I believe in the holy, catholic church':

> 15.56[38] And now, having spoken of Jesus Christ, our Lord, only Son of God, we continue by saying that we also believe in the Holy Spirit, so that the Trinity which is God may be complete. Then we mention the Holy Church. This gives us to understand that the intelligent creation which is the free Jerusalem is to be subordinated in order of speech to the Creator, that is, the supreme Trinity; for anything that is said of the man Christ has reference to the unity of the person of the only-begotten.

[37] Text PL 42.1085

[38] Text: PL 40.258; cf. *St. Augustine, Faith, Hope and Charity,* ACW 3.58.

The just order of the Creed demanded that the Church should come next after the Trinity as a house after its dweller, a temple after its deity, a city after its founder. The whole Church is to be understood here, not only that part which is on pilgrimage on the earth, from the rising of the sun to the going down thereof, praising the name of the Lord and singing a new song after its old captivity, but also that part which is always in heaven, which always remained loyal to God, its creator, and did not experience the woe that springs from a fall.

Cyprian's teaching on baptism and its relationship to the Church as mother (cf. *On Unity* 6, ep. 74.7) is echoed later by Augustine in his treatise, *Against Julian* (Julian was a dissident bishop of Eclanum):

3.17[39] Next for some reason you invoke the example of Abraham and Sara, which I think I have fully answered. You forgot something and wanted to add it when you remembered it, a human enough thing which happens frequently, so let us hear it. You say: "A prophecy is now being fulfilled in the region of Africa: neither the spouse nor the chastity of the beautiful, holy woman, who was a figure of the Church, was safe but by divine help she was there preserved unharmed." I shall not waste time on your many words. You address the one to whom you are writing and say: 'We must pray God, blessed Turbanus, brother, fellow-priest, that the powers remain constant even in this storm, and that He delay not to preserve the Catholic Church, the mature, fruitful, chaste, comely bride of His Son, from abduction into Africa or from Africa by Manichaean brigands.' This is likewise our own prayer against Manichaeans, and Donatists, and other heretics, and against all enemies of the Christian and Catholic name who may be found in Africa.

[39] Text: PL 44.; cf.FOTC 35.134

Baptism, the link of the People of God

Are we then, brigands come out of Africa against you because in opposition to you, a pest come to us from overseas, and a pest to be conquered by Christ, the Saviour, we bring forward one martyr from here, Cyprian, through whom we prove we are defending the ancient Catholic faith against the vain, profane novelty of your error? What perversity! Did the Church of God located in Africa need your prayers when most blessed Cyprian proclaimed the truths you are attacking? Were they lacking when he said: 'Much more ought nobody forbid baptism to a new-born infant who has committed no sin except that, since he has been born in the flesh according to Adam, he has contracted the ancient death's contagion in his first birth, so that not his own but another's sins are remitted for him' (ep.64.5) When Cyprian learned and taught these things did he need your prayers to preserve Sara unharmed in the region of Africa, and to deliver the beauty of the Church from being abducted by the Manichaeans, who by your reasoning deceived Cyprian himself before the name of Manichaeus was heard from Roman soil? See what monstrous, frenzied charges you make against the very ancient Catholic faith in your inability to find anything else to say.

Irenaeus is thinking along the same lines in *Against the Heresies*: 1. 10,2[40]

The Church, having received this preaching and this faith, although she is disseminated throughout the whole world, yet guarded it, as if she occupied but one house. She likewise believes these things as if she had but one soul and one and the same heart; she harmoniously proclaims and teaches them, and hands them down, as if she possessed only one mouth. For, although the languages of the world are diverse, nevertheless; the authority of the tradition is one and the same.

[40] Text: SC 264.158

OTHER CHRISTIAN COMMUNITIES

#15 *The Church knows that she is joined in many ways to the baptized who are honored by the name of Christian, but who do not, however, profess the Catholic faith in its entirety or have not preserved unity or communion under the successor of Peter.*

Cyprian, in writing to Quirinus, provides a cluster of Scriptural texts which taken together offer a basis for ecumenical re-appraisal between the Roman church and other Christian churches:

> 86 [41] That a schism must not be made, even though he who withdraws should remain in one faith and in the same tradition. In Solomon, in Ecclesiastes, 'He who chops wood is in danger from it, if the iron becomes dull' (Eccl. 10:9). And in Exodus: 'in one house it shall be eaten; you shall not cast forth the flesh abroad out of the house (Ex. 12). Also in Psalm 133: 'Behold, how good it is, and how pleasant, where brethren dwell at one! (Ps. 133:1). Also in the Gospel of Matthew: 'He that is not with me is against me, and he that gathereth not with me scattereth' (Mt. 12:30). Also in the First Epistle of Paul to the Corinthians: 'I beg you, brothers, in the name of our Lord Jesus Christ, to agree in what you say. Let there be no factions; rather, be one in mind and in judgment. And in Psalm 67: 'God, who makes men to dwell with one mind in a house' (Ps.67:6).

Optatus of Mileve, in his *On the Donatist Schism*, is in no doubt about the most likely base for Christian unity:

> 2.2[42] You cannot deny that you know that in the city of Rome the episcopal chair was first conferred on Peter, on which Peter, the head of the apostles, sat, whence he was also called Cephas, and on this one chair unity is preserved by all.

[41] Text: CCL 111.1.164   [42] Text: CSEL 26.36

RELATIONS WITH NON-CHRISTIANS

#16 Those who have not yet received the Gospel are related to the People of God in various ways.

It would be disingenuous to pretend that an ecumenical spirit prevailed in the early Christian church. It is all too easy to document a virulent anti-semitism in many of the early christian writers like Melito of Sardis, Tertullian and John Chrysostom. What dialog there was merely aimed at converting orthodox Jews to Christianity by proving the divinity of Christ from the Scriptures and insisting that the new Israel, the Church, had replaced the old, the synagogue, in the divine dispensation. This is evident in such works as the *Dialog between Timothy and Aquileia* and the better-known *Dialog with Trypho* of Justin Martyr.

Justin's exchange is with 'a Hebrew of the circumcision, a refugee from the recent war (the 132-135 revolution against Hadrian in Palestine), at present a resident-alien in Corinth (c.1). The Dialog is not without acrimony and anti-semitic overtones, but it does start from the promising enough common ground that as much can be gained from philosophy as from the Law and the Prophets in that God is a prominent subject in philosophical discourse which constantly proposes questions about his unity and his divine providence. In fact, the task of philosophy is defined (c.1) as 'inquiry about the divine'.

This is a sample of Justin's approach to the Jew, Trypho:

> 58.[43] I have no skill in artistic arrangement of argument, but I have received one grace from God — to understand his scriptures — and I invite everyone to share freely and abundantly in this grace, lest I should be held accountable at the judgment.

THE MISSIONARY CHURCH

#17 Go, therefore, and make disciples of all nations...
(Jn.20:21)... The Church has received this solemn command of Christ from the apostles...accordingly she never

[43]Text: PG 6.605

ceases to send heralds of the Gospel until such time as the infant Churches are fully established, and can themselves continue the work of evangelization. ... Each disciple of Christ has the obligation of spreading the faith to the best of his ability.

The missionary challenge inherent in a text like *From the rising of the sun even to its setting my name is great among the Gentiles* (Mal.1:11), has early resonances in the *Didache*, in Justin Martyr, and in Irenaeus.

The *Didache* has the earliest description of the Sunday Eucharist:

> c.14[44] On the Lord's Day, after you have assembled, break bread and offer the Eucharist, having first confessed your offences, so that your sacrifice may be pure ... For it was said by the Lord: 'In every place and time let there be offered to me a clean sacrifice.'

Justin Martyr, in his *Dialog with Trypho*, quotes Mal. 1:10-12 and comments:

> 41[45] By making reference to the sacrifices which we Gentiles offer to Him everywhere, the eucharistic bread and the eucharistic chalice, He predicted that we should glorify His name.

Irenaeus characterizes the Eucharist as the new oblation of the New Covenant:

> IV.17,5[46] Again, giving directions to His disciples to offer to God the first-fruits of His own created things... He took that created thing, bread, and gave thanks and said, This is my body. And the chalice, likewise, which is part of that creation to which we belong, He confessed to be His blood, and taught the new oblation of the new covenant, which the Church, receiving from the apostles, offers to God throughout all the world.

[44]Text: SC 248.192   [45]Text: PG 6.564   [46]PG 7.1023

III

The Church Is Hierarchical

A VARIETY OF MINISTRIES

#18 ...he [*Jesus*] *put Peter at the head of the other apostles and in him he set up a lasting and visible source and foundation of the unity both of faith and of a communion.*

Clement of Alexandria called Peter 'the chosen, the pre-eminent, the first of the disciples' (*What Rich Man*,21). Origen says: "Peter, who has received upon himself the building of the Church based upon the Word, and who is so confirmed in goodness that the gates of Hell will not prevail against him (*Against Celsus*, 6.77). Basil the Great, writing *Against Eunomius*, says:

> 2.4[1] When we hear the name Peter (or Rock) we must not interpret it materially but in virtue of the properties which it suggests. We should understand it of the son of Jonas called from the trade of fishing to the apostolic ministry who because he excelled in faith received the building of the church upon himself.

Gregory of Nazianzus is equally clear on Peter's role:

> 32.18[2] Peter is called from the chief among the apostles and entrusted with the foundations of the church.

---

[1] Text: PG 29.577   [2] Text:PG 36.193

John Chrysostom calls Peter 'the ever-fervent, the leader of
the apostolic choir' (hom.54.2 *on Matt.*) and elsewhere
salutes him as 'the leader of the choir, the mouthpiece of the
apostles, the head of the *phratria*, the chief of the whole
world, the foundation of the Church, the ardent lover of
Christ.'[3]
Augustine calls him (s.147,2): 'a figure of the unity of all
shepherds' (PL 38.798).

*This teaching concerning the institution, the permanence,
the nature and import of the sacred primacy of the Roman
Pontiff and his infallible teaching office, the sacred synod
proposes anew to be firmly believed by all the faithful...*

Ignatius of Antioch, in the Preface to his *Epistle to the
Romans*, calls the Church at Rome 'a Church without blemish which holds the primacy of the community of love' (SC
10.106).

   The most detailed history of the early Roman pontificate
is provided by Eusebius of Caesarea, *Ecclesiastical History*.
First we are told (h.e.3.1) that 'after the martyrdom of Peter
and Paul the first man after Peter to be appointed bishop of
Rome was Linus.' Later we are told that Linus held office
for twelve years and was succeeded by Anancletus in 80
A.D., and the third to succeed was Clement. Hegesippus, a
second century writer on whom Eusebius is obviously very
dependent as a source, made a journey by sea from the East,
possibly from Jerusalem, to Corinth and Rome, during
which he was in close association with very many bishops,
'receiving the same teaching from all.' 'But when I came to
Rome', Hegesippus says in the quotation in Eusebius,
(H.E.4.22) ' I made a succession list as far as Anicetus....
And from Anicetus Soter received the succession'. Whatever about the precise meaning of succession (Gk. *diadoche*) — and the term was undoubtedly used for political
successions as well as for continuities in the philosophical
schools — it is clear that for both Eusebius and Hegesippus,
in the search for sound, uncontaminated Christian teaching
the best hope reposed in an unbroken sequence of episcopal

[3]PG 56.274

leaders in the major ecclesiastical sees, a sequence that was felt to be unbroken from the time of the apostles.

Primacy and Infallibility of Roman Pontiff

Vatican II reiterates one of the main teachings of Vatican I, the Primacy and Infallibility of the Roman Pontiff. Cyprian, in his treatise on *The Unity of the Church*, makes the Petrine office the foundation and principle of unity:

> 4[4] Proof of faith is easy in a brief statement of the truth. The Lord speaks to Peter: "I say to thee", He says, "thou art Peter, and upon this rock I will build my church, and the gates of hell shall not prevail against it. And I will give to thee the keys of the kingdom of Heaven; and whatever thou shalt bind on earth shall be bound also in Heaven, and whatever thou shalt loose upon earth shall be loosed also in Heaven" (Mt. 16:18,19). Upon him, being one, He builds His Church, and although after His resurrection He bestows equal power upon all His Apostles, and says, 'As the Father has sent me, I also send you' Receive ye the Holy Spirit: if you forgive the sins of anyone they are forgiven; if you retain the sins of anyone they are retained' (Jn. 20:21,23), yet, so that He might display unity, He established by His authority the origin of that same unity as originating from one. Surely, the rest of the apostles also were that which Peter was, endowed with an equal partnership of office and of power, but the beginning proceeds from unity, that the Church of Christ may be shown to be one.

THE COLLEGIALITY OF THE APOSTLES

#19 *The Lord Jesus...appointed twelve to be with Him whom He might send to preach the kingdom of God. These apostles He constituted in the form of a college or permanent assembly, at the head of which He placed Peter, chosen from among them.*

[4]Text:OECT, ed., Bévenot, 60(2nd edition)

Eusebius, in his *Ecclesiastical History*, tells us that our Lord and Saviour not long after the beginning of His ministry, called the twelve apostles, and these alone of all his disciples he named 'apostles' as an especial honor (1.10). For Irenaeus they are the twelve pillars of the Church, corresponding to the twelve tribes of Israel (*a.h.* 4.21,3). In Valentinian gnosticism, Irenaeus reports (2.14,8), the twelve aeons emanated from Anthropos (Man) and Ecclesia (Church). Clement of Rome invoked the Old Testament type of the twelve tribes in his *Letter to the Corinthians*:

> 43.2[5] For, when the priesthood had become an object of jealousy and the tribes were quarrelling as to which of them had been honored with that glorious dignity He ordered the leaders of the twelve tribes to bring Him each a rod....

There was no shortage of other prototypes in the Old Testament for the Twelve: the twelve bells attached to the robe of the Highpriest (cf. Justin, *Dial.* 42), the twelve gates of Sion (Ps. 87:2), on which Augustine comments in his *In Ps.86*:

> [6] Do not imagine that the gates are one thing, the foundations another; Why are the Apostles and Prophets foundations? Because their authority supports our weakness. Why are they gates? Because through them we enter the kingdom of God. ... And twelve gates of Jerusalem are spoken of, and the one gate is Christ. And the twelve gates are Christ, for Christ dwells in the twelve gates, hence; twelve was the number of the apostles. (*Enarr. in Ps.*)

St. Jerome, in his *Against Jovinian*, writes:

> 1.26[7] But, you say, the Church was founded upon Peter although elsewhere the same is attributed to all the apos-

---

[5]Text: SC 167.170   [6]Text: CCL 39.1201   [7]Text:PL 23.247

tles, and they all receive the keys of the kingdom of Heaven and the strength of the Church depends upon them all alike; yet one among the twelve is chosen so that when a head is appointed there may be no occasion for schism.

St. Gregory the Great, in his *Book of Sacraments* says there is a liturgical Preface which speaks of 'your apostles in whom you are exceedingly glorified, through whom you assemble the sacred body of your only-Begotten and in whom you set up the foundations of your church". Another Preface speaks of 'the apostolic foundations of the church' in celebrating the solemnity of blessed Thomas the apostle, 'one of their college' (PL 78.51,152).

St. Hilary of Poitiers says that despite the denial of Peter and the fear and flight of the apostles, because of their good-will, they were so perfect that they became the foundations and pillars of the Church. (PL 9.450).

THE BISHOPS - SUCCESSORS OF THE APOSTLES

#20 The apostles were careful to appoint successors in this hierarchically constituted society.

Eusebius of Caesarea, in the Preface to his *Ecclesiastical History*, announces in his very first sentence that it is his purpose 'to hand down a written account of the successions of the holy Apostles...and of the number of those who were illustrious guides and leaders in especially prominent dioceses.' Toward the end of the same chapter he says he will be 'happy if we succeed in rescuing the successions, if not of all, at least of the most renowned, of the Apostles of our Saviour in those churches which even today are accounted pre-eminent.' The Churches which he concentrates on throughout the first seven books of his *History* are Jerusalem, Antioch, Alexandria, and Rome, though he frequently gives successions elsewhere, e.g. Smyrna and Caesarea. In this concern for succession lines of bishops he has often been accused of anachronism, projecting back into the second century the highly developed hierarchical system that characterized the church of his own day.

It is clear, however, from his quotations from earlier writers-Hegesippus and Irenaeus, in particular — that apostolic succession was already a matter of considerable concern in the second century. Here we present two quotations from Eusebius which he took from Hegesippus and Irenaeus, and one from Tertullian, with whose work, since the latter wrote in both Greek and Latin, Eusebius was fairly familiar.

> 4.22,1[8] Now, Hegesippus, in the five treatises that have come down to us, has left us a very complete account of his own opinion. In these he shows that he travelled as far as Rome and mingled with a great many bishops and that he received the same doctrine from all. It is well to listen to what he said after some remarks about the epistle of Clement to the Corinthians (see further, 4.23; 3.16). 'And the church of the Corinthians remained in the true word until Primus was bishop of Corinth. I associated with them on my way to Rome and I spent some days with them in Corinth, during which we were mutually stimulated by the true Word. And while I was in Rome I made a succession up to Anicetus, whose deacon was Eleutherus, and Soter succeeded Anicetus, and after him Eleutherus. In each succession and each city all is as the Law, the Prophets and the Lord preach.'

Eusebius tells us (4.21 SC31.199) that Hegesippus is a contemporary of Irenaeus "from whom the sound and orthodox faith of the apostolic tradition has come to us in writing". He is referring chiefly to his *Against Heresies*, or, to give it its better title, *The Detection and the Overthrow of the False Gnosis*. In a single chapter (3.23) Eusebius quotes from Books II and III of *Against Heresies* on the subject of the apostolic traditions. 'And all the presbyters who had associated with John, the disciple of the Lord, attest to John's tradition, for he remained with them until the times of Trajan' (=adv.h.2.22,15). 'Moreover, the Church at Ephe-

---

[8]Text: SC 31.199

sus which was established by Paul and where John remained with them until the times of Trajan, is a true witness to the tradition of the Apostles' (= adv.h. 3.3.4).

Another key text on apostolic succession is provided by Tertullian, *On the Prescription of Heretics*. On the question of whether truth or heresy had chronological priority Tertullian suggests that the answer is already provided (cf. Mt. 13:24) in the parable of the sowing by the Lord of the good seed of the wheat but its later adulteration by its enemy, the devil, with the useless weed of the wild oats. He continues:

> c.32[9] Now if there are any heresies which are daring enough to claim that they originated in the apostolic age, thereby insinuating that they were handed down by the apostles, because they existed in the time of the apostles, we would simply say: Let them produce the original documents of their churches; let them unroll the scroll of their bishops, running down in due succession from the beginning so that the bishop will be able to point for his ordainer and predecessor a man of the apostles or an apostolic man who continued in good standing with the apostles. For that is how the genuine apostolic churches keep their records, for instance the church of Smyrna, which records that Polycarp was appointed there by John, as also the church of Rome, which shows Clement having been similarly ordained by Peter. In exactly the same way the other churches show their leaders appointed to their episcopal offices by apostles and regarded as transmitters of the apostolic seed. Let the heretics devise some similar arrangement. For they will stop at nothing after their original blasphemy. But no amount of connivance will improve their cause.

Amongst those various offices...the chief is held by the function of those who, through their appointment to the dignity and responsibility of bishop, and in virtue conse-

[9]Text: SC 46.130

quently of the unbroken succession, going back to the beginning, are regarded as transmitters of the apostolic line.

Ignatius of Antioch, whose letters have been described as the epiphany of the monarchical episcopate, writes on his way to martyrdom in Rome toward the end of Trajan's rule as emperor (98-117) *to the Church at Smyrna*:

> 8[10] You must all follow the lead of the bishop, as Jesus Christ followed that of the Father.
> Where the bishop appears, there let the people be, just as where Jesus Christ is, there is the Catholic Church.

And to the church at Ephesus he wrote:[11]

> 6. Obviously, anyone whom the Master of the household puts in charge of his domestic affairs ought to be received by us in the same spirit as He who has charged him with this duty. Plainly, then, one should look upon the bishop as upon the Lord himself.
> 3.2 Surely, Jesus Christ, our inseparable life, for His part is the mind of the Father, just as the bishops, though appointed throughout the vast, wide earth, represent for their part the mind of Jesus Christ.
> 4.1 It is proper for you to act in agreement with the mind of the bishop and this you do. Certainly your presbytery, which is a credit to its name, is a credit to God; for it harmonises with the bishop as completely as the strings with a harp. This is why the praises of Jesus Christ are sung in the symphony of your concord and love.

That bishops are the successors of the apostles is stated in Clement's *Epistle to the Corinthians*:

> 44[12] Our Apostles also knew, through our Lord Jesus Christ, that there would be contention over the bishop's

---

[10]Text:SC 10.138   [11]Text: SC 10.62,60   [12]Text: SC167,168,172

office. So, for this reason, having received complete fore-knowledge, they appointed the above mentioned men, and afterwards gave them a permanent character, so that, as they died, other approved men should succeed to the ministry.

Earlier in the same epistle we read:

42.4 Preaching, accordingly, throughout the country and the cities they appointed their first-fruits, after testing them by the Spirit, to be bishops and deacons of those who should believe. And this they did without innovation, since many years ago things had been written concerning bishops and deacons. Thus, the Scripture says in one place: I will establish their bishops (*episkopous*) in justice and their deacons in faith (cf. Isa. 60:17)

Irenaeus of Lyons is an equally clear witness to the idea of an apostolic succession of bishops in his *Against Heresies*:

111.31[13] It is within the power of all, therefore, in every Church who may wish to see the truth, to contemplate clearly the tradition of the apostles manifested throughout the whole world; and we are in a position to reckon up those who were by the apostles instituted bishops in the churches, and to demonstrate the successions of these men to our own times.

The twin notions of succession (Gk. *diadoche*) and tradition (Gk. *paradosis*) were basic to the early church's understanding of what differentiated orthodox and heretical churches. Two quotations from earlier writers in Eusebius, *Church History* will illustrate this.

The first is from a lost work of Clement of Alexandria, called *Hypotyposeis or Outlines*:

2.1.4[14] After the Resurrection the Lord gave the tradition of knowledge to James the Just, and John, and Peter, and

[13] Text: SC34.100   [14] Text:SC 31.49

these gave the tradition to the other apostles, and the other apostles to the Seventy, one of whom was Barnabas.

The other is a better-known text from *Against Heresies* of Irenaeus:

5.6.5[15] Having founded and built the church (of Rome) the blessed apostles entrusted the episcopal office to Linus, who is mentioned by Paul in the Epistles to Timothy (cf. 2 Tim. 4:21); Linus was succeeded by Anancletus; after him, in the third place from the apostles the bishopric fell to Clement, who had seen the blessed apostles and conversed with them, and still had their preaching ringing in his ears and their authentic tradition before his eyes...

Clement was succeeded by Evarestus, Evarestus by Alexander; then Xystus was appointed, the sixth from the apostles, followed by Telesphorus, who suffered glorious martyrdom; next came Hyginus, then Pius, and after him Anicetus. Anicetus was succeeded by Soter, and now, at the twelfth stage from the apostles, the position is filled by Eleutherus. In the same order and the same succession (*diadoche*) the authentic tradition (*paradosis*) received from the apostles and passed down by the Church, and the proclamation of the truth, have come down to us.

THE FULLNESS OF PRIESTHOOD

#21 ...*the fullness of the sacrament of Orders is conferred by episcopal consecration, that fullness, namely, which both in the liturgical tradition of the Church and in the language of the Fathers of the Church is called the high priesthood, the acme of the sacred ministry.*

[15]Text: SC 41,31.

The Apostolic Tradition has very precise details on the election, confirmation and consecration of bishops:

> 2.[16]Let the bishop be ordained, being in all things without fault, chosen by all the people.
>
> And when he has been proposed and found acceptable to all, the people shall assemble on the Lord's Day, together with the presbytery and such bishops as may attend.
>
> With the agreement of all, let the bishops lay hands on him and the presbytery stand by in silence.
>
> Let all observe silence, praying in their heart for the descent of the Spirit. Then, at the request of all, let one of the bishops standing by impose hands on the candidate for episcopacy, praying over him:

Prayer of episcopal consecration

> God and Father of our Lord, Jesus Christ, Father of mercies and God of all consolation, (2 Cor.1:3) who dwells on high and regards the humble (Ps. 112:5-6), who knows all things before they occur (Dan.13:42) you who have predestined from the beginning the just race from Abraham, having instituted the rulers and priests and have not left your sanctuary without ministry, you have been well pleased to be glorified from the beginning from the foundation of the earth in those whom you have chosen. Now pour forth that power which comes from you, the power of the sovereign Spirit which you have given to your beloved son, Jesus Christ, which he has given to your holy apostles who have founded the church everywhere as your sanctuary for the glory and unceasing praise of your name.
>
> Grant, Father who knows hearts, to your servant whom you have chosen for the episcopacy, to feed your holy flock and to exercise in your regard the primacy of priesthood without reproach in his service night and day, that he may make your sight propitious unceasingly and

---

[16]Text: ed.,Botte, *La tradition apostolique*, SC11,2nd ed.,1968,40

offer the gifts of your holy church, and that he may have, in virtue of the spirit of supreme priesthood, the power to remit sin in accordance with your commandment (cf. Jn. 20:23), and to distribute orders according to your command, and may he please you by his gentleness and his cleanness of heart, offering to you the odor of sweetness by your infant, Jesus Christ by whom to you be glory, and power and honor forever and ever, Amen.

The sacramental nature of episcopal ordination is insisted upon by Leo the Great in one of the sermons preached by him on the anniversary of his own ordination:

> s.5[17] And so, beloved, we confess that although Jesus sits at the right hand of God the Father, the Chief Priest is not lacking from the congregation of his priests and rightly he is sung to by the lips of the whole church and of all his priests: Thou art a Priest forever according to the order of Melchisedech (Ps. 109:4). For he is the true, eternal priest whose administration can have no diminution or end.

The earliest liturgies make clear that the ordination of bishops gives them the triple power to sanctify, to teach and to rule. In the *Leonine Sacramentary* the prayer is[18]:

> Fulfil in your priests the summit of your mystery, and sanctify them, appointed with the adornments of all glorification and the flow of heavenly anointing. Grant to them the episcopal chair to rule your church and all the people. May you be to them authority, power and steadfastness.

The active role of the laity in electing a bishop was more in evidence in the pre-Constantinian church than later when considerations like piety and democratic choice were replaced by more mundane ones.

---

[17] Text: CCL 138.23   [18] Text: ed. C. Mohlberg, 1956, 119-120

The *Didache* lays down a general principle:

> c.15[19] You must, then, elect for yourselves bishops and
> deacons who are a credit to the Lord, men who are gentle,
> generous, faithful and well-tried. For their ministry to
> you is identical with that of the prophets and teachers.

Likewise the *Apostolic Constitutions* (c.360) invokes apostolic authority for insisting that 'a man who is to be consecrated bishop should be blameless in every respect and
elected by the people; (Book VIII, Section II, IV.)

As late as the time of St. Severin, the 'Apostle of Noricum'
(= modern Austria), we know from his biographer, Eugip-
pius, that he was elected bishop by popular choice:

> 21,1-2:[20] Paulinus, a priest, had come to St. Severin,
> ...wishing to go home, he was told by him: 'Hurry,
> venerable priest, for soon, my beloved friend, you will be
> adorned by the dignity of episcopal rank, much as the will
> of the people — so we believe — may be against your
> wish'. Paulinus had hardly come home when the words of
> the prophet concerning him were fulfilled. For the citi-
> zens of Tiburnia, which is the metropolis of Noricum,
> forced him to accept the eminency of being their high
> priest.

THE COLLEGIALITY OF BISHOPS

*#22 Just as...St. Peter and the rest of the apostles constitute a
unique apostolic college, so in like fashion the Roman
Pontiff, Peter's successor and the bishops, the successors of
the apostles, are related with and united to one another.*

One of the most welcome theological developments at
Vatican II was the new emphasis on the fact that the church
was governed by the apostolic college, consisting of Pope
and bishops. Without weakening the Roman Church's

---

[19]Text: SC 248.192   [20]Text: PL 62.1185 (VII.28)

claim to primacy — it is still, in Ignatius' felicitous phrase, 'a church without blemish, which holds the primacy of the community of love' (*Ad Rom.,* pref.)—the new collegiate, more democratic, emphasis is on shared responsibility.

Irenaeus eloquently describes the unanimous agreement that should characterize the teaching of the catholic church:

> 1.10,2[21] The Church, having received this preaching and this faith, although scattered throughout the whole world, yet as if occupying but one house, carefully preserves it. She also believes these teachings, as if she had but one soul, and one and the same heart, and she proclaims them and teaches them, and hands them down with perfect harmony as if she possessed only one mouth.

Cyprian of Carthage, in a famous letter to Pope Stephen of Rome (254-257 A.D.) calling on him to intervene in a disputed matter, explicitly uses the term 'college':

> 68,3 [22] For that reason, dearly beloved brother, the large body of bishops is joined by the bond of mutual concord and the chain of unity, so that if anyone of our college should attempt to engage in heresy, and wound and lay waste the flock of Christ, the others, as useful and merciful shepherds, should assist and should assemble the sheep of the Lord into the flock.... For although we shepherds are many, yet we feed one flock; and all of the sheep whom Christ sought by His blood and passion we ought to collect and to cherish....

Cyprian's strong feelings on collegiality were crystallized in a single sentence in the *De unitate*, c. 5: 'The authority of the bishops forms a unity, of which each holds his part in the totality'.

The collegiality of bishops in Cyprian's day is obvious from one of his *Letters*:

[21] Text: SC 264.158   [22] Text: CSEL 111,2.746

ep.56.3[23] Yet, since you wrote that I should treat of this matter most fully with very many colleagues and since so important a subject demands greater and more deliberate counsel from the discussion of many, and since now almost all, at the start of the Paschal season, are remaining at home among their brethren, when they have satisfied their obligation of celebrating the festival among their own people and have begun to come to me, I shall treat with each of them more fully that there may be a strong stand on the subject about which you sought advice, and the firm judgment of many bishops deliberated in the Council may be reported back to you.

The emphasis on agreement arrived at after conciliar deliberations is also evident from Eusebius, *Church History*. A letter to Cyprian of Carthage from Dionysius of Alexandria brings good news about the abatement of persecution and a weakening of support for the Novatian heresy:

VII.5[24] Now let me assure you, brother, that all the previously divided churches in the East and still farther away have been united and all their prelates everywhere are in union, overjoyed at the return of peace. (He names seven bishops, giving their sees.). . . . I have named the more distinguished bishops only, for fear of prolixity. However, the whole of Syria and Arabia. . . . Mesopotamia, Pontus and Bithynia — in a word, everyone everywhere is delighted at the new spirit of harmony and brotherly love. . . .

It is worth noting that as late as the end of the fourth century, when John Chrysostom is eulogising the city of Rome, he praises it as the city of the twin pillars of the Church, Peter and Paul. In his *Homilies on Romans* he says:

32[25] I love Rome for this reason particularly, although indeed there are other grounds for praising it — its great-

[23]Text: CSEL 112,2,649   [24]Text: SC 41.168   [25]Text: PG 60.678

ness, its antiquity, its beauty, its populousness, its power, its wealth, its successes in war. But, passing over all these other reasons, I esteem it as blessed on this account, that even in his lifetime Paul wrote to them, and loved them so much, and talked with them in person, and brought his life to a close there. That more than anything else makes the city noteworthy. Like a great, strong body it has the bodies of these two saints like two glistening eyes.

Theodoret, bishop of Cyrus, near Antioch, wrote to Leo, Bishop of Rome, in the same collegial spirit in which Paul appealed to Peter:

ep.113[26] If Paul, the herald of truth, the trumpet of the Holy Spirit, had recourse to the great Peter in order to obtain a decision from him concerning those at Antioch (Acts 15:1-35), much more do we, small, humble folk, run to the apostolic throne to get healing from you for the woes of the churches. For it is fitting that in all things you should have the primacy, seeing that your See possesses many special advantages. Other cities get a reputation for size, or beauty, or population, or some that are devoid of those advantages are compensated by certain spiritual advantages: but your city has got an abundance of blessings from the great Provider. Moreover she is specially adorned by her faith, testified to by the apostle, saying, 'your faith is spoken of throughout the world'(Rom. 1:8).... In her keeping too are the tombs...of our common fathers and teachers, Peter and Paul... They have rendered your see most glorious; this is the crowning achievement of your blessings....

#23 *Collegiate unity is also apparent in the mutual relations of each bishop to individual dioceses and with the universal Church.*

The mutual concern of bishops for churches often far distant from their own sees is dramatically obvious in the

[26]Text: SC 111.56

surviving letters of such distinguished Fathers as Athanasius, Basil, and Gregory Nazianzus. Athanasius, after being deposed from his see of Alexandria and replaced by the Arian, Gregory, in 339, wrote an 'encyclical' letter to his 'fellow-ministers in every place', to inform them that:

> [27]...the members of the whole Church are seen divided from one another...the Arian madmen glory in the plunder of churches, while the people of God, and the clergy of the Catholic Church, are compelled either to have communion with the impiety of the Arian heretics or else to forbear entering in amongst them.

In his *History of the Arians*, Athanasius protests against the despotic interference of the Arian emperor, Constantius, in ecclesiastical matters and he stakes an uncompromising claim to separation of church and state:

> [28]For if a judgement has been passed by bishops, what concern has the emperor with it? Or if it was only a threat of the emperor, what need in that case was there of the so-called bishops? When was such a thing heard of before from the beginning of the world? When did a judgement of the church derive its validity from the emperor? Or, rather, when was his decree ever recognized by the Church?

This collegiate spirit, very obvious in the case of Basil the Great, can be illustrated by a letter of his to Athanasius which illustrates too that Athanasius was in turn a role model for him in this regard:

> 69[29] Although it is quite enough for most men to watch over their own responsibilities, this does not suffice for you. On the contrary, you have as great a care for all the churches as for the particular one entrusted to you by our benign Lord. For indeed you never cease reasoning,

[27]Text:PG 25.233   [28]Text: PG 25.756   [29]Text: LCL, ed. Deferrari, 11.38

admonishing, writing, and, on every occasion, sending the best counsellors.

How well Basil succeeded in emulating the universal concerns of Athanasius is evident from the Panegyric preached at his funeral by his life-long friend, Gregory of Nazianzus:

> 41[30] When his local affairs were settled...his designs became more ambitious and assumed a loftier range. For while all others had their eyes on their own immediate concerns and their own territories, he, a moderate in all else, could not be a moderate in this, but, with head erect and casting his mental eye around, encompassed the whole world which had been traversed by the Word of salvation.

Under the stress of heretical factions, Basil clearly perceived the benefits of collegiality and church unity between East and West. Writing to the great Athanasius, bishop of Alexandria, he says:

> ep. LXVI[31] In comparing the present (disorder of the churches) with the past you can see how utterly different the present situation is from the past. You can easily conclude that, if our situation continues to deteriorate at the present rate nothing will prevent the churches from being completely changed in a short time to some other structure...I have also known and realized for long from my modest understanding of our affairs that the one way of maintaining our churches is union with the Western bishops. If they were willing to show for the dioceses in our region that zeal which they displayed in the case of one or two in the West who were discovered to be heretical, it would perhaps be to our advantage and mutual interests, since our rulers are looking askance at the trustworthiness of the people, and the people everywhere are following their bishops without question.

---

[30]Text: PG 36.549   [31]Text: LCL 11.26

We see him acting as an effective go-between in a true spirit of collegiality in his letter to Meletius, bishop of Antioch:

> ep.CXX[32] I received a letter from Bishop Eusebius, dearly beloved, enjoining us to write again to the Western bishops concerning certain ecclesiastical matters, and he wanted me to write a letter to be signed by all who are in communion. But since I could not see how I was capable of writing about the matters in his instructions, I am sending the memorandum to you, your Reverence, so that you yourself, after reading it and listening attentively to the reports from the most beloved brother, Sanctissimus, our fellow presbyter, may consent to write about these matters as you think fit. We are ready to subscribe to your letter and have it quickly transmitted to those in communion so that the one who is to go to the Western bishops may set out with all the signatures.

In a letter unaddressed, but generally believed to have been sent to Damasus, bishop of Rome, he writes:

> ep.LXX[33] ...For, what could be more pleasing than to see men who are separated by such distances bound in a union of love into one harmonious membership in the body of Christ? Almost the whole East, most honorable Father, (and by the East I mean the regions from Illyricum to Egypt) is being shaken by a mighty storm and deluge. The old heresy, sown by Arius, the enemy of truth, is now shamelessly springing up, like a bitter root yielding deadly fruit, and is finally prevailing. For, as a result of calumny and abuse, the champions of sound faith in each diocese have been banished from the Church, and the control of affairs has been handed over to those who are leading captive the souls of purest faith. We have awaited one solution of the difficulties — the visitation of your Mercifulness. Indeed, in times past,

---

[32] Text:LCL 11.244   [33] Text: LCL 11.48, ed. Deferrari

your incredible charity has always attracted us and we for a short time regained strength in our soul because of the joyful report that we should have a visitation from you. But, we are utterly disappointed in our hope.

St. Basil, in *Letter 90,* To the most holy brothers and bishops of the West, lets forth a sustained cry of anguish at the state of church affairs in the East and begs their prayers and consoling help:

> ep.90[34]Affairs here are in a distressing condition, most honorable brothers. The Church, like a boat in the middle of the sea buffeted by the constant onslaught of the waves, has been reduced to complete exhaustion by the incessant attacks of her opponents, failing some speedy intervention of God's goodness. Therefore, just as we esteem as a personal blessing the agreement and union among you, so also we implore you to show compassion to us in our disagreements, and not to sever yourselves from us merely because our countries are far distant, but since we are united in the sharing of the Spirit, rather admit us to the harmony and unity of one body.
>
> Our afflictions are well known and do not need to be recounted; they already have been trumpeted forth to the whole world. The teachings of the Fathers have been despised; the traditions of the Apostles are set at naught; the crafty inventions of innovators have been introduced into the churches; men now are skilful rhetoricians rather than theologians; worldly wisdom takes priority and the glory of the cross relegated. The shepherds are expelled and fierce wolves introduced in their place, who rend asunder the flock of Christ. The houses of prayer are emptied of their former congregations; the deserts are full of mourning people....
>
> If there is any consolation of love, any communion of the Spirit, any feelings of pity, bestir yourselves to come to our relief. Employ zeal in the pursuit of piety, rescue us

[34]Text: LCL 11.124

from this storm. And let that blessed dogma of the Fathers be spoken fearlessly among us, that dogma which confounds the hateful heresy of Arius and builds up the churches on the sound doctrine in which the Son is acknowledged to be consubstantial with the Father, and the Holy Spirit is numbered with them and adored with equal honor, in order that your fearlessness in defence of the truth, God's gift to you, and your glorying in the confession of the divine and saving Trinity may also be bestowed upon us with the help of your prayers and your co-operation.

Eusebius in his *Church History* gives us more than one example of far-sighted bishops whose concerns for the Church did not stop at their own diocesan boundaries:

4.23[35] First, it must be said of Dionysius (of Corinth) that when he had been enthroned as Bishop of Corinth he lavished his inspired industry unstintingly, not only on those under him, but also on those in foreign lands, rendering the greatest service of all in the general epistles which he discharged to the Churches.

The seven extant 'encyclical' letters of Dionysius were sent to such distant destinations as Crete, Sparta, Athens, Nicomedia, Pontus and, very interestingly, Rome, and he tells the Romans that the letter sent earlier from the Church of Rome by Clement is still read in his Church on Sundays.

John Chrysostom writes in his *In Praise of Eustathius*:[36]

And he (Eustathius, bishop of Antioch) did not confine his pastoral care to his own flock, but he sent out people everywhere to teach, exhort, discuss, and to close off the enemy. For he was so well taught by the grace of the Spirit that he felt it was not enough to be solicitous about the church to which he was appointed by the Holy Spirit

[35]Text: SC 31.202   [36]Text: PG 50.602

to preside over, but wherever in the whole world it was established. That he had gathered from his holy prayers.

The bishops of Spain write in a collegiate fashion to Pope Honorius after the Sixth Council of Toledo in 638. Apparently the Pope had written to them to chide them for not being relentless enough in the struggle to extirpate heresy. They show no obsequiousness in defending their own handling of what was for them a local problem. The reply is Epistle 21 in the Letters of Braulio of Saragossa:

21[37]...for we, bishops of all Spain and of Gallia Narbonensis had met in common assembly when...there was brought to us your decree in which we were urged to be more robust on behalf of the faith and more eager in wiping out the pernicious heresies of the perfidious....

On our part, we are not wrapped up in such a degree of sloth as to forget our duty or not to be moved by the prospect of the inspiration of heavenly grace, but, according to the demands of the times, we have had a planned distribution of speakers; we would have your blessedness know that the fact that the matter has not been completely settled by now is due to indulgent, rather than timid or negligent, action following the advice of the apostle, saying: "With modesty admonishing those that follow a different wisdom: in case God should give them repentance to know the truth, and they recover themselves from the snares of the devil" (2 Tim.2:25-26). Therefore, we desired to act with calculated restraint...and to temper our genuine severity with the continuous and lengthy treatment of preaching....

The unjust arguments used by your holiness to criticize us have absolutely nothing to do with this case, if I may say so; especially that quotation from Isaia (and not from Ezechiel as you stated, although all the prophets prophesize with one spirit), "Dumb dogs, they cannot bark" (Isa. 56:10), does not pertain to us at all....

[37]Text: PL 80.668

HIERARCHY AND *DIAKONIA*

#24 *That office, however, which the Lord committed to the pastors of his people is, in the strict sense of the term, a service...a diakonia.*

Origen's reminder is always salutary: 'he who is called to the episcopacy is called, not to domination, but to the service of the whole church' (hom. VI in Isa., PG 13.239). He returns to this thought in his *Commentary on Matthew*:

> XI.15[38] Accordingly, if we do alms before men...we receive the reward from men (cf. Mt. 6:1-4); in general, everything done with an eye on being glorified by men has no reward from Him who...rewards those who act in secret. So, too, those influenced by thoughts of vain glory or love of gain act with sullied motives. The teaching which is thought to be the teaching of the church, if it becomes servile through words of flattery, either when it is used as a pretext for avarice, or when one seeks human glory because of one's teaching, it is no longer the teaching of those 'who have been set up in the church: first, apostles, second, prophets, third, teachers (1 Cor, 12:28). And you will say the same with regard to one who seeks the office of bishop for the sake of human esteem, or for the sake of gain received from converts to the word who give in the name of piety; a bishop of that sort assuredly does not 'aspire to a noble task' (1 Tim. 3:1), nor can he be 'irreproachable, temperate, self-controlled', as he is intoxicated with glory and intemperately puffed up with it. The same also is applicable to presbyters and deacons.

Ignatius of Antioch delineates the ideal bishop in writing to the Philadelphians:

> 1.[39] I know that your bishop received the ministry (*diakonian*) which makes for the common good neither from himself nor through men, nor for vain-glory, but through

---

[38] Text: PG 13.953   [39] Text: SC 10.120

the love of God the Father and the Lord Jesus Christ.
And I am amazed at his gentleness, and at his ability to do
more by silence than those who use vain words. For he is
attuned to the commandments as a harp to its strings.
Therefore, my soul blesses his godly mind, recognizing its
virtue and perfection, and the unruffled and dispassion-
ate temperament by which he lives in complete god-like
gentleness.

THE BISHOP AS TEACHER

#25 *Among the more important duties of bishops that of
preaching the Gospel has pride of place.*

A striking example of the importance of the preaching office
is shown by Augustine's testimony to the effectiveness of the
preaching of Ambrose in the *Confessions*:

> V.13,23[40] When, therefore, the officials of Milan sent to
> Rome, to the prefect of the city, to ask that they provide
> them with a teacher of rhetoric for their city and to send
> him at the public expense, I applied for the job through
> these same persons, drunk with the vanities of the Mani-
> chaeans, to be freed from whom I was going away....
> They recommended that Symmachus, who was then per-
> fect, after I had satisfied him in an audition, should
> appoint me. And to Milan I came, to Ambrose, the
> bishop, famed through the whole world as one of the best
> of men, thy devoted servant. His eloquent discourse in
> those times abundantly provided your people with the
> flour of your wheat, the gladness of your oil, and the
> sober intoxication of your wine. To him I was led by You
> without knowing it, so that by him I might be led to You
> in full knowledge.

Admittedly Jerome is less enthusiastic about Ambrose's
talents when he writes in his *On Illustrious Men*, 124, "of
him, since he is still alive, I will reserve my judgment, lest I

---

[40] Text: CCL 27 (1981), 70

be blamed either for flattery or for speaking the truth', and, in a backhanded compliment to Basil of Caesarea, he also accused Ambrose of writing bad things in Latin taken from good things in Greek.

St. Basil, in his *Homily on Psalm 28*, describes the teaching office as follows:

> 28.2[41] Like the rams leading the flocks are the leaders of Christ's flock. They lead them forth to the blooming, fragrant nourishment of spiritual doctrine, water them with living water with the help of the Spirit, raise them up and nourish them until they produce fruit. Then they guide them to rest and safety from those who lay snares for them.

For bishops are preachers of the faith. Authentic teachers, that is, teachers endowed with the authority of Christ, who preach to the people committed to them the faith they must believe and put into practice.

The job description of a bishop in the *Constitution of the Holy Apostles* starts off on the right note of service or *diakonia* even though it turns dangerously near to apotheosis in the end:

> 2.26[42] The bishop is the minister of the Word, the keeper of knowledge, the mediator between God and you in the various parts of your divine worship. He is the teacher of piety, and next after God he is your father, who has begotten you again to the adoption of sons by water and the Spirit. He is your ruler and governor; he is your king and potentate; he is, next after God, your earthly God, who has a right to be honored by you.

Chrysostom's audience were not always as receptive, or as positive, as he would like them to be. In *Homily III on 2*

---

[41]Text: PG 29.284

[42]Text: F.X.Funk,Didascalia et Constitutiones Apostolorum, 105.

Thessalonians he reprimands them for complaining that there is a certain sameness to the Sunday homily:

> 2 [43]Why is it necessary to have a homily? Everything in the Scripture, you say, is clear and open; what is necessary is also obvious. But because you derive pleasure from listening you seek after this. But, tell me, with what pomp of words did St. Paul speak, and yet he conquered the world. Or what about the unlettered Peter? But I know not, you say, the things that are contained in the Scriptures. Why? Are they spoken in Hebrew? Are they in Latin or in a foreign language? Aren't they in Greek? But, you say, they are obscurely expressed. What is obscure? Tell me. Are they not narratives? For you doubtless know the obvious parts since it is about the obscure parts that you inquire. There are numerous narratives in the Scriptures. Tell me any one of these. But you cannot. These things are an excuse, mere words. Every day, you say, is the same story. What about the theatres, do you hear the same thing there? Do you not see the same things on the race-course? Isn't everything the same? Is it not the same sun that rises daily? Is it not the same food that you use? ... When you say that you hear the same things every day I would like to ask you: tell me, from what prophet was the reading taken just now? From what apostle, what epistle? Now you cannot tell me; you seem to hear strange things . . . . If they are the same you ought to know them. "The same things", you say, "are always said." These are simply words that spring from sloth and are self-serving.

#26. *In each altar community, under the sacred ministry of the bishop, a manifest symbol is to be seen of that charity and "unity of the Mystical Body, without which there can be no salvation."*

The bishop as 'the steward of the grace of the supreme priesthood' has an especially important role with regard to

[43]Text: PG 62.485

the Eucharist. As Ignatius of Antioch put it: 'You must
follow the lead of the bishop as Jesus Christ followed that of
the Father.... Let that celebration of the Eucharist be
considered valid which is held under the bishop or anyone to
whom he has committed it' (*Ep. ad Smyr.,* 8, SC10.138).
And in his *Epistle to the Ephesians* Ignatius says:[44]

> Come together in common, one and all without excep-
> tion in charity, in the grace which comes from his name,
> in one faith and in one Jesus Christ, who is of the race of
> David according to the flesh, son of man and Son of God,
> so that with undivided mind you may obey the bishop
> and the priests, and break one bread which is the medi-
> cine of immortality and the antidote against death, ena-
> bling us to live forever in Jesus Christ.

We get a vivid description of the role of the president of
the Eucharist in Justin Martyr's *First Apology* in the course
of his description of the Sunday liturgy:

> 67[45] Then we all rise together and pray, and as we said
> already, when our prayer is ended, bread and wine and
> water are brought, and the president in like manner offers
> prayers and thanksgivings according to his ability and the
> people assent, saying Amen; and there is a distribution to
> each, and a participation of that over which thanks have
> been given, and to the absent a particle is sent by the
> deacons.
>
> And they who are well-off, and willing, make a contri-
> bution as they see fit, and what is collected is deposited
> with the president, who helps the orphans and widows,
> and those who, because of sickness or whatever cause are
> in need, and those who are in bonds, and strangers
> sojourning among us, and in a word cares for all in need.

Tertullian refers to the same practice of dispensing the

---

[44]Text: SC 10.76   [45]Text: PG 6.429

proceeds of collections at the beginning of his *To the Martyrs*:

> 1 [46]Blessed martyrs elect, along with the nourishment for the body which our Lady Mother the Church from her breast, as well as individual brethren from their private resources, furnish you in prison, accept also from me some offering that will contribute to the sustenance of your spirit. For it is not good that the flesh be feasted while the spirit goes hungry.

Tertullian is also an excellent source on the role of the bishop in Baptism and Eucharist. The following text is all the more interesting in that it comes from a work belonging to his Montanist period called *The Chaplet*:

> 3.2[47]. . . Let us, then, investigate the question whether or not a tradition without a written source should be accepted. The answer will certainly be 'No' if we cannot produce examples of other observances which are without written source in Scripture and rest solely on the basis of tradition and yet have come to have the force of custom.
>
> To begin, for example, with baptism: When we are about to enter the water, and, as a matter of fact, even a short while before, we declare in the presence of the congregation before the bishop that we renounce the devil, his pomps and his angels. After which we are immersed in the water three times, making a somewhat fuller pledge than the Lord has prescribed in the Gospel. After this, having stepped from the font, we are given a taste of a mixture of milk and honey, and from that day, for an entire week, we forego our daily bath. We also receive the sacrament of the Eucharist which the Lord entrusted to all at the hour for Supper, at our early morning assemblies, and then from the hand of none but

[46]Text: CCL 1.3   [47]Text: CCL 2.1042

the bishops. Further, we make offerings for the dead on their anniversary to celebrate their birthday (of eternal life)...

4. Now, if you demand a precise scriptural precept for these and other practices of church discipline, you will find none. Tradition, you will be told, has created it, custom has strengthened it, and faith has encouraged its observance.... Therefore, from these few examples, it will be clear that, because of its being observed, a non-written tradition also can be defended, if it is confirmed by custom, which is itself a valid witness to an approved tradition from the mere fact that it has gone on for a long time.

The bishop, then, pre-eminently is the president of the Eucharist at the local congregations of the faithful called Churches or assemblies. The prominence of growth in faith and charity in such a community exercise is obvious in the early Mozarabic eucharistic prayer:

About to receive, brethren, into mortal entrails a heavenly sacrifice, and into the cubicle of a human heart the Lord host, let us cleanse our consciences from every trace of vice so that there may be nothing of guile or pride in us, but that the whole brotherhood may be joined in the pursuit of humility and the assent of charity so that with confidence we may deserve to say from earth: Our Father, Who art in Heaven. (PL 96.759B)

EPISCOPAL POWER

#27 *The pastoral charge..is entrusted to them fully, nor are they to be regarded as vicars of the Roman pontiff; for they exercise the power which they possess in their own right.*

Ambrose of Milan illustrates how a certain independence in local practice is not inconsistent with deep loyalty to the See of Peter. In his *On the Sacraments* he is discussing local

practice in the matter of washing the feet on Holy Thursday
at the liturgy:

> 111.5[48] We are not unaware of the fact that the Church in
> Rome does not have this custom, whose character and
> form we (i.e. in Milan) follow in all things. Yet Rome
> does not have the custom of washing the feet. Note,
> therefore: perhaps this practice declined because of the
> crowds. Yet there are some who say, and try to allege in
> excuse, that this should not be done in the mystery, or in
> baptism, or in regeneration, but that footwashing should
> be done simply as for a guest. But the one has to do with
> humility, the other with sanctification. Finally, realize
> that the mystery is also sanctification. 'If I do not wash
> your feet, you shall have no part with me'. So I have this
> to say, not to rebuke others, but to commend my own
> ceremonies. In all things I desire to follow Rome, yet we
> too have human feeling; what is preserved more rightly
> elsewhere we too preserve more rightly.

Very many years later an acerbic Irish missionary would
make the same distinction between this basic loyalty and
incidental differences in writing to a Roman pontiff.
Columbanus to Pope Boniface IV:

> ep. 5[49]. . .So it is not for vainglory or for impudence that
> I, a creature of the meanest station, dare to write to such
> exalted men; grief rather than pride drives me to sug-
> gest. . .that the name of God is blasphemed among the
> Gentiles through your mutual contest. . . .
> 3. Indeed I grieve, I confess, for the disgrace of St. Peter's
> chair. . . I shall speak as a friend, disciple, and close
> follower of yours, not as a stranger; therefore I shall
> speak out freely, saying to those that are our masters and
> helmsmen. . . . Watch, for the sea is stormy and whipped
> up by fatal blasts. . . . Watch, for water has now entered

[48]Text: SC 25.94

[49]Text: PL 80.275; cf. Scriptores Latini Hiberniae, ed. G.S.M.Walker,38

the vessel of the Church, and the vessel is in perilous straits.

For all we Irish, inhabitants of the world's edge, are disciples of Saints Peter and Paul and of all the disciples who wrote the sacred Canon by the Holy Spirit; and we accept nothing outside the evangelical and apostolic teaching; none has been a heretic, none a Judaizer, none a schismatic; but the Catholic Faith, as it was delivered by you first, who are the successors of the holy apostles, is maintained unbroken.

Of particular interest on the question of diversity in unity is a reply of Gregory the Great to Augustine of England:

XI.64[50] Although there is only one Faith, the customs of the various Churches differ, and mass is celebrated in one way in the holy Roman church and in another way in the churches of Gaul....

You, brother, know the usage of the Roman Church in which you were brought up: hold it very much in affection. But as far as I am concerned if you have found something more pleasing to almighty God, either in the Roman, or in the Frankish, or in any other Church, make a careful choice, and institute in the Church of England, which is as yet new to the Faith, the best usages which you have accumulated from many churches.

For we should love things not because of their places of origin; rather we should love places because of the good things they contain. Therefore choose from each particular Church what is godly, religious and sound, and dishing it all together serve it on the English table for the regular menu.

The governing role of the bishop is clear from the so-called *Pseudo-Clementines*:

h.3.64[51] But if you absolutely refuse to be regarded as the holder of an administrative office, then you are appar-

---

[50]Text: PL 77.1186   [51]Text: GCS 42.80

ently unaware that the recognized status of the president is very helpful in keeping the multitude in check; for everyone obeys the office-bearer, since he is under the obligation of conscience to do so. And is it not sufficiently clear to you that you do not have to wield the sceptre as do secular rulers, but rather as a servant who ministers to them, as a father who cares for them, as a physician who visits them, as a shepherd who watches over them — in a word, as one who is totally involved in their well-being?

The author goes on to point out that the greater the difficulty in governing the Church of Christ, the greater the reward, and that obedience on the part of the governed is just as important as the right dispositions in those governing:

66. Your work, then, is to command what needs to be done, that of the brethren to be acquiescent and not to disobey. If they acquiesce then they will be saved; if they continue in disobedience, then they will be punished by Christ, for the president acts in the place of Christ. Therefore to dishonor the president is to dishonor Christ, and, through Christ, God. This is said to show the brethren the danger into which disobedience of the elders may lead them. For he who disobeys your commandment resists Christ, and he who disobeys Christ makes God angry. 67. The Church, as a city built upon a hill (cf. Mt.5:14) must have an order pleasing to God and to good administration. At ove all, the bishop as the authoritative, leading spokesman must be heard. The elders have to see that these orders are carried out. The deacons should walk about, looking after the bodies and souls of the brethren, and report to the bishop.

Governing by Counsel and Example

St. Gregory the Great, in his *Pastoral Care*, stresses the importance of good example on the part of bishops if they are to govern well:

2.3[52] The ruler should be exemplary in his conduct, that by his manner of life he may show the way of life to his subjects and that the flock, following the teaching and conduct of the shepherd, may proceed the better through example rather than through words. For the one who, in virtue of his position, must propose the loftiest ideals is bound *ipso facto* to be himself an embodiment of these ideals. His voice penetrates the hearts of his hearers all the more readily if his way of life commends what he says. What he enjoins in words will be translated into practice by the help of his example.

Gregory of Nazianzus gives us a vivid impression of the excitement, not to say intrigue, surrounding elections:

h.18.33[53]The city of Caesarea was in turmoil over the election of a bishop. One had just died and his successor was being sought, and there arose a violent dissension that could not easily be resolved. The city was naturally inclined to be especially factious in this matter because of the fervor of its faith, and the splendor of the see only increased the rivalry. Such were the circumstances, and several bishops were at hand to consecrate the candidate chosen. The multitude was split up into many factions, all proposing different candidates and, as usually happens in such cases, as one happened to be influenced by friendship for a particular candidate or by piety toward God. Finally, the whole people, with one accord, selected by force one of their leading citizens, a man of the loftiest character, but one who had not yet been sealed with holy baptism; brought him though reluctant to the bishops and with threats and entreaties begged that he be consecrated.

The choice of the laity similarly prevailed in the case of a person still unbaptized in the case of Ambrose of Milan and Synesius, who became bishop of Cyrene in Tunisia, North

---

[52]Text: PL 77.28   [53]Text: PG 35.1028

Africa, largely as a result of his reputation as a neo-Platonist scholar and his diplomatic skills on a legation to Constantinople in 399.

Even Leo the Great, whose ecclesiastical tendencies were centripetal, stressed the need for consultation in the selection of bishops:

> ep.10[54] The wishes of the congregation and the testimony of the people should certainly be waited for; the opinions of the nobles and the choice of the clerics should be asked for: these are the procedures ordinarily observed in the consecrating of bishops by those who know the decrees of the Fathers.

Elsewhere (ep. 167) Leo says[55]:

> No consideration allows making bishops of those who have not been chosen by the clerics, sought for by the people, and consecrated by the provincial bishops with the consent of the metropolitan.

THE OFFICE OF PRIEST

#28 *...in virtue of the sacrament of Orders...they are consecrated in order to preach the Gospel and shepherd the faithful as well as to celebrate divine worship as true priests of the New Testament.*

The ideal priest is depicted in Polycarp's *Epistle to the Philippians*, which he sent them to accompany a copy of the *Epistles of Ignatius*, shortly after the latter's death:

> 6 [56] The presbyters must be tenderhearted, merciful toward all, guiding back the sheep that have gone astray, visiting all the sick, not neglecting the widow, or orphan, or poor man, but always taking thought for that which is

[54]Text: PL 54.632   [55]Text: PL 54.1203
[56]LCL, *The Apostolic Fathers*, 1.290

honorable in the sight of God and of man (cf.2 Cor.8:21) refraining from all anger, respect of persons, unrighteous judgment, being removed from all love of money, slow to believe anything evil against anyone, not hasty in judgment, knowing that we are all debtors because of sin.

Gregory the Great, in his *Pastoral Care*, says of priests:

11.3[57] Therefore, by divine ordinance, the priest receives a shoulder for sacrifice and that, too, the right one and separate (cf. Exod.29:22). His conduct should be not only profitable but outstanding. He should not only do what is upright in the midst of the wicked but also surpass the well-doers among his subjects, and as he surpasses them in the dignity of his rank so should he in the virtue of his conduct.

In John Chrysostom's great classic, *On the Priesthood* the dignity of the office of priesthood is especially associated with the privilege of offering sacrifice:

111.4[58] For the office of the priesthood is executed on earth but it ranks among things that are heavenly and with good reason; for it was neither a man, nor an angel, nor an archangel, nor any created power, but the Paraclete Himself that established this order, and commanded that men still in the flesh should imitate the functions of angels. ... For the priest stands bringing down not fire (like Elias; cf. IIK 18:23-40) but the Holy Spirit, and he prays long, not that fire may descend from heaven and consume the offerings, but that grace may descend upon the victim, and through it inflame the souls of all and render them brighter than silver tried in fire.

In an unusual document, *On the State of the Church*[59], written around 1100 by Gilbert, Bishop of Limerick, the

---

[57]Text: PL 77.28; cf. ACW 11.48-49   [58]Text: SC 272.142
[59]Text: PL159.1000.

first Papal Legate to Ireland, the duties of priests are item-
ised as follows:

> The duties of priests are fourteen in number: to take
> charge, to be subject, to pray, to offer, to preach, to teach,
> to baptize, to bless, to excommunicate, to reconcile, to
> anoint, to give communion, to commend souls to God, to
> bury the dead. We must be specific about each of these.
> *To take charge* is the priest's job: to act as discerning
> judge in individual cases, to enjoin a penance with justice
> and mercy, and to counsel with gentleness. *To be subject*
> is to serve the bishop with humility of soul. *To offer* is the
> priest's duty: to sacrifice bread and wine with water daily,
> and on Holydays to have the Te Deum, the Benedictus
> and the Magnificat, and before the Sacrifice to incense
> above and around the altar and the sacrifice. Let the
> Deacon, however, incense the altar before the Gospel. *To
> pray* also is the priest's duty: to adore and supplicate God,
> to praise Him for His admirable works, to bless Him, to
> give Him thanks for His benefits, and to ask for future
> blessings. All of this is especially discharged in *celebrat-
> ing the Mass* and the canonical Hours, and since this
> cannot be dealt with briefly it will be discussed later. *To
> preach* is the priest's duty: to summon Jews, infidels or
> catechumens to the grace of baptism, and to recall here-
> tics to the Catholic faith. *To baptize* belongs to the priest:
> to baptize with threefold immersion in the sacred font
> those who are exorcized and believe, confessing the Holy
> Trinity. This, like Mass, ought to be done in church,
> except in case of necessity. And the sacrifice of the Body
> and Blood of the Lord is often made, in memory of His
> Passion, as He Himself prescribed, saying: This is My
> Body and My Blood: Do this in memory of Me, as often
> as you consume (cf. 1Cor.11: 24,25). Baptism, however, is
> not repeated, lest the invocation of the Holy Trinity be
> thought ineffectual, because Christ died once for our sins
> (1 Pet.3:18) *To teach* is the priest's task: to instruct the
> baptized how they are fortified by humility against pride,
> by lowliness against inane glory, by benevolence against

envy, by modesty against anger, by joy against sadness, by generosity against avarice, by abstinence against gluttony, and by chastity against lust. For these eight vices, and everything that stems from them, although not sins in themselves are always suggestive of sin, that is inviting consent.

But as long as the soul does not consent to them it commits no transgression but rather gains a crown. The priest's teaching role includes preaching every Sunday on what days of the week the faithful ought to abstain and have a feria. The priest can *bless*, in the presence of the bishop, water and salt on Sundays; he can bless a meal, and bridegroom and bride, and those going to read the Lessons, apart from the Gospel, and judgment water, and bread etc. . . . And in the bishop's absence he can bless a cleric's tonsure, or a widow's veil, or new fruits, candles on the Purification of Holy Mary, ashes on the head of one going to read the Gospel, and the people at the Dismissal. He can sprinkle blessed water to bless new houses and other new things. It is the duty of the priest *to excommunicate* those relapsed into crimes from which they have been recalled once, twice, three times, and to eliminate from communion with the faithful the nonpenitent, so that there may be no communion with them either in way of life or in converse. It is the priest's duty *to reconcile*: to receive into the unity of the faithful, with the bishop's consent, however, those in danger of death repenting their crimes. The priest can *anoint* any of the faithful once in any grave illness because the holy anointing often gives relief not only of soul but of body. The priest ought *to give communion* immediately to the baptized, and to all the faithful three times a year (at Easter, Pentecost, and Christmas), and to those nearing death, if they ask for it by word or sign, or if one of the faithful testifies that they have previously asked. The priest ought *to commend* by prayers *the souls of the faithful* departing their bodies, and to remember them frequently in Mass and in prayer. Although forgiveness is promised the sinner at whatever hour he repents, nevertheless some

punishment awaits the sinner, namely the fire of purgatory, which receives for complete purgation those who
have just left the body and have not been fully purged by
the laments of penance, whatever is done for them by way
of prayer and almsgiving is profitable for their purgatory,
for the perspiration of the living is the repose of the dead.
The last duty of the priest is *to bury the corpses of the
faithful.* He should personally spread clay three times
over the corpse with a spade saying, *from clay you have
fashioned me.* And let there be other places adjacent to
the cemeteries of the saints in which are buried the bodies
of the faithful drowned or killed, because commending
their souls to God is not prohibited. But the bodies of
infidels and criminals must be interred far from those of
the faithful; we do not communicate in death with those
with whom we do not communicate in life.

THE OFFICE OF DEACON

#29 *At a lower level of the hierarchy are to be found deacons,
who receive the imposition of hands 'not unto the priesthood
but unto the ministry'.*

The *Didache* specifies the requirements for good bishops
and deacons:

> 15 [60] Accordingly, elect for yourselves bishops and dea-
> cons, men who are an honor to the Lord, of gentle
> disposition, not attached to money, honest, and well-
> tried, for they too render you the sacred service of the
> prophets and teachers. Do not, then, despise them; for
> they are your dignitaries together with the prophets and
> teachers.

It should be noted about this text that there is no reference
to presbyters, and that the bishops do not seem to enjoy any
more exalted role than the prophets and teachers who are

[60]Text: SC 248.192

mentioned more frequently throughout the *Didache*.

In the *Didascalia Apostolorum* deacons are told to imitate the example of charity and brotherly love shown to us by Christ when He washed the feet of the apostles at the Last Supper:

> XVI[61] If then Our Lord did this, will you, O deacons, hesitate to do the same for those who are weak and infirm, you who are the workmen of the truth, and carry the likeness of Christ? Do you therefore minister with love, and do not murmur or hesitate; otherwise you will have ministered , so to speak, for men's sake, and not for the sake of God, and you will receive your reward according to your ministry in the day of judgment.

We get further insight into the somewhat pedestrian functions of deacons from the *Constitutions of the Holy Apostles*:

> 11.58[62] And if, after people have taken their seats, any other person enters, one who enjoys some standing and reputation in the world, either from abroad or from your own country, you, bishop, if you are proclaiming the Word of God, or listening to the cantor or reader, are not to interrupt the Word of God to receive him personally and find a place up front for him. Instead, you should continue unruffled, without interrupting your discourse or your concentration. Let the brethren receive him through the intervention of the deacons. And if there is no vacant place, let the deacon orally but not angrily ask some inferior to vacate his place for the stranger. Indeed it is only reasonable that one who loves the brethren should spontaneously make room. If he refuses, however, let the deacon move him forcibly, and set him down at the very back, that the rest may learn to give place to the more distinguished. And even if the one arriving is a poor

[61] Text: ed. R.H. Connolly, 151

[62] Text: F.X. Funk, ed. *Didascalia et Constitutiones Apostolorum,* 1.169; cp. ANF7.422

man, from a poor family, or a stranger, whether young or old, if there is no place, let the deacon find a place no less for these, and with enthusiasm, so that his ministry before God may be well-pleasing, in that he is no respector of persons. The deaconesses shall do as much for the women, whether poor or rich, who happen to arrive unexpected.

The rights and duties of deacons are quite circumscribed in the *Constitutions of the Apostles*:

> VIII.28,4 The Deacon does not bless. He does not give a benediction but receives it from the bishop and the priest. He does not baptize. He does not offer (sacrifice). However, when the bishop or priest has offered, he gives it to the people, not acting as a priest, but ministering to the priests. (Funk, 530)

We may fittingly conclude this section with a description of an early church assembly which outlines in some detail the various roles played by bishop, priest, deacon and layperson in a service of worship. This description comes from the *Constitutions of the Holy Apostles*. The work in its present form probably dates to around 400 A.D., but it contains a collection of earlier regulations for ecclesiastical discipline, law and liturgy and some of its elements are as old as the *Didache*.

> II.VII.57[63] Be thou, O bishop, holy and blameless. Do not resort to blows, or anger, or cruelty. Rather build up, convert, teach. Be forbearing of evil, of gentle mind, meek, long-suffering, ready to exhort, ready to comfort, a man of God. When you call an assembly of the Church, like a pilot of a huge ship, appoint the assemblies to be held with all possible skill charging the deacons, as mariners, to prepare places for the brethren, as for passengers, with all due care and decorum.

[63] Text: F.X.Funk, ed., *op. cit*, 159; cf.ANF7.421

First, let the place of assembly be long, with its top facing East, with vestries on both sides at the East end, and so resembling a ship. Let the Bishop's throne be placed in the center, and on each side of him let the presbyters take their seats. Let the deacons stand near at hand, in close, tight-fitting garments, for they are like the mariners and deck-hands of the ship. Let the laity sit on the other side, in silence and good order. And let the women sit separately, also in silence.

Let the reader stand on a raised eminence in the center and read from the books of Moses, Joshua, son of Nun, from Judges, Kings, and Chronicles, and from the books composed after the return from Captivity, and, besides these, from the books of Job and Solomon, and from the sixteen Prophets. And when two lessons have been read from each, let somebody else intone the hymns of David, and let the people join in the conclusions of the verses. Afterwards let there be a reading from Acts and from the epistles of Paul, our fellow-worker, which he sent to the churches under the guidance of the Holy Spirit. After that let a Deacon or a Presbyter read the Gospels, both those which Matthew and John have delivered to you, and those which the fellow-workers of Paul, Luke and Mark, received and left to you. And while the Gospel is being read, let the presyters, deacons and laity all stand, in complete silence, for it is written: 'Be silent, and hear, O Israel, (Deut. 27:9). And again, 'But do thou stand there and listen'(Deut. 5:31).

Next, let the presbyters one by one, not all together, exhort the people, and let the bishop do so last of all, in that he is the commander. Let the porters stand at the men's entrances and keep them under observation. Let the deaconesses likewise stand at the women's entrances, like mariners. For the same description and pattern was to be found in the tabernacle of the testimony and in the temple of God.

And if anybody is found sitting out of place, let him be rebuked by the deacon, as a manager on shipdeck, and be sent back to his assigned place; for the church is not only like a ship but also like a sheepfold. Just as the shepherd separates the goats and the sheep according to type and age, yet all run together, like to like, so it is in the Church. Let the young people sit by themselves, if there is place for them; if not, let them stand. But let elderly citizens sit in order. As for the children who stand, let their fathers and mothers take them to them.

Let the younger women also sit by themselves, if there is place for them; but if there is not, let them stand behind the other women. Let married women who have children be placed by themselves; but let virgins, widows and elderly women stand, or sit, in front of the others. And let the deacon be the one who allocates places, so that every one who comes in may go to the appropriate place, with nobody allowed to sit at the entrance. Likewise, let the deacon supervise the people, so that there is no whispering, or slumbering, or laughing, or nodding, for everyone in church ought to stand wisely, soberly and attentively, with attention fixed upon the word of the Lord.

After this, let all rise up of one accord, and looking toward the East, after the catechumens and penitents have been dismissed, pray to God in the East, He who ascended Eastward to the heaven of heavens, remembering also the ancient situation of Paradise in the East, from where Adam, when he had yielded to the allurements of the serpent, and disobeyed the command of God, was expelled.

As to the deacons, after the prayers have been completed, let some of them attend upon the offering of the Eucharist, ministering to the Lord's body with reverence. Let others keep watch on the people, ensuring silence. But let that deacon standing next to the high priest say to the people, Let no one have any quarrel with his neighbor; let no one come in hypocrisy. Then let the Lord's kiss be exchanged, men with men, women with women. But let no one do it deceitfully, as Judas betrayed the Lord with a kiss.

After this let the deacon pray for the whole Church, for the whole world and its various parts — for the priests and rulers, for the high priest and the Emperor, for the peace of the universe. After this, let the high priest pray for peace upon the people, and bless them, as Moses commanded the priests to bless the people in these words: 'The Lord bless you, and keep you; let the Lord make His face to shine upon you, and give you peace.'

Let the Bishop pray for the people and say: 'Save Thy people, O Lord, and bless Thine inheritance which Thou hast obtained with the precious blood of Thine Anointed One, and hast called a royal priesthood, and a holy nation (1 Pet. 2:9).

After this, let the sacrifice follow, the people standing and praying silently, and when the offering has been made, let every rank separately partake of the Lord's Body and precious Blood, approaching in order and with reverence and holy awe, as to the body of their king. Let the women approach with heads covered, as is becoming the rank of women. And let the door be kept under observation, lest any infidel, or one not yet initiated, should come in.

IV

The Laity

ALL THE FAITHFUL SHARE THE CHURCH'S MISSION

#30 *Everything that has been said of the People of God is addressed equally to laity, religious and clergy.*

In St. Paul's injunction: we must all practice the truth in love (Eph 4:15) there is no distinction between clergy and laity. All are called to Christian perfection. The Greek word for 'layman', *laikos*, unknown in the New Testament, is first found in Christian literature in Clement of Rome's *Epistle to the Corinthians*:

> 40,5[1] Special functions are assigned to the high priest: a special office is imposed on the priests; and special ministries are allocated to the Levites. The layman is bound by the rules laid down for the laity.

Ignatius of Antioch clearly has the three orders of hierarchy, presbytery and laity in mind in his *Epistle to the Ephesians:*

> 4[2] Hence it is proper for you to act in agreement with the mind of the bishop; and this you do. Certainly your presbytery, which is a credit to its name is also a credit to

[1]Text: SC167.166   [2]Text: SC 10.60

God, for it harmonises with the bishop as completely as the strings with a harp. That is why in the symphony of your concord and love the praises of Jesus Christ are sung.

In the *Didascalia* the laity are instructed[3]:

Reverence bishops who deliver you from sin, who by water bring you to rebirth, who fill you with the Holy Spirit, who nourish you on the Word as milk, who bring you up in doctrine, who strengthen you in teaching, make you partake of the holy Eucharist of God, and make you partakers and joint heirs of God's promise.

Diversity of the Laity

In a homily on the Deuteronomy text, 'Give heed to yourself, lest perhaps a wicked thought steal in upon you' (Deut. 15:9), Basil the Great comments on the diversity of occupations among the Christian laity and on how they can best employ their talents in the service of the Church:[4]

Acquire an exact understanding of yourself, that you may know how to make a suitable allotment of each of the two sides of your nature: food and clothing to the body, and to the soul the doctrines of piety, training in refined behavior, the practice of virtue, and the correction of vice....

Every one of us, indeed, who is instructed in the Holy Scripture is the administrator of some one of those gifts which, according to the Gospel, have been apportioned to us. In this great household of the Church not only are there vessels of every kind of gold, of silver, of wood and of clay (cf. 2 Tim. 2:20) — but also a great variety of pursuits. The house of God, which is the Church of the living God, has hunters, travellers, architects, builders, farmers, shepherds, athletes, soldiers. To all these this short admonition will be appropriate, for it will produce

[3] Text: ed. Connolly, 94   [4] Text: PG 31.205

in each proficiency in action and energy of will.

You are a hunter sent forth by the Lord who says, 'Behold, I send many hunters and they shall hunt them upon every mountain'(Jer. 16:16). Take good care, therefore, that your prey does not elude you, so that, having captured them with the word of truth, you may bring back to the Savior those who have been made wild and savage by iniquity. You are a traveller, similar to him who prayed, 'Direct my footsteps' (Ps.118:133). 'Give heed to yourself' that you swerve not from the path, that you deviate neither to the right nor to the left (cf. Deut. 17:20). Keep to the King's highway. The architect should lay the firm foundation of faith which is Jesus Christ, and let the builder look to his materials: not wood, or hay, or stubble, but gold, silver, precious stones (cf. 1 Cor. 3:11-12).

If you are a shepherd, take care that none of your pastoral duties is neglected. And what are those duties? To bring back that which was lost, to bind up what was broken, to heal what was diseased (cf. Ezech. 34:16). If you are a farmer, dig around the unfruitful fig tree and administer remedies that will increase fertility. If a soldier, 'labor with the gospel, war a good warfare '(2 Tim. 1:8, 1 Tim. 1:18) against the spirits of wickedness. Take unto yourself all the armor of God against the desires of the flesh. Do not entangle yourself in secular affairs that you may please the one who has enlisted you (2 Tim. 2:4). If you are an athlete, 'give heed to yourself' lest you violate any of the laws for athletes, for no one is crowned if he does not compete lawfully. Like Paul, run, fight, and strike with the fist (1 Cor. 9:26). Keep the eye of your soul unwaveringly alert, like a skilful boxer. Shield your private parts with your hand. Keep your gaze fixed on your opponent. In the race, stretch forward to the things that are before (Phil. 3:13). So run that you may win (1 Cor. 9:24); do battle with your invisible adversaries. That is the sort of person this precept would like you to be as long as you live, neither losing heart nor resting, but soberly and vigilantly keeping a watch over yourself.

Origen maintained that a priesthood is given to the whole Church of God and to all who believe. When God said to Moses on Sinai, 'if you hearken to my voice and keep my covenant, you shall be my special possession...a kingdom of priests, a holy nation' (Exod.19:5) he in effect made us all a consecrated people, a priestly, worshipping people. John Chrysostom says the same thing: 'You are yourself made a priest in Baptism...a priest in that you offer yourself to God (*On 2 Cor.* PG 61.417).

#31   *The term "laity" is here understood to mean all the faithful except those in Holy Orders and those who belong to a religious state approved by the Church. That is, the faithful who by Baptism are incorporated into Christ, are placed in the People of God, and in their own way share the priestly, prophetic and kingly office of Christ, and to the best of their ability carry on the mission of the whole Christian people in the Church and in the world.*

It can be seen from this definition that baptism is the necessary rite of initiation to membership of the People of God, and that 'laity' is the comprehensive term for all so initiated who have not advanced to Holy Orders or membership of a religious order. The fact that membership of the laity also involved sharing the priestly, prophetic and kingly offices of Christ was understood from the beginning but sometimes led to exaggerated claims. Tertullian, in his *Exhortation to Chastity*, for instance, strikes a very topical note for the present age characterized by a shortage of priests:

> 7.3[5] But where no college of ministers has been appointed, you, the laity, must celebrate the eucharist and baptize; in that case you are your own priests, for where two or three are gathered together, there is the Church, even if these are lay people.

[5]Text: CCL 2.1025

Here is it important to note that this work belongs to the last two decades of Tertullian's life, after he joined the Montanists, a sect which emphasized spontaneous ecstatic enthusiasm and the exercise of prophecy untrammelled by hierarchical surveillance. Augustine later found it necessary to deny to the laity the right and duty of celebrating the Eucharist here granted to them by Tertullian.

In ep. III,8[6] Augustine writes:

> These virgins in the land of their captivity are like the Israelites in that land where they could not offer sacrifice to God, as they were accustomed to do. These also cannot make an offering at the altar of God, nor find there a priest to make their offering to God for them.

And in s.116:[7]

> ...if he recognizes such a one he will dispense through the ministry of his priests to him His body and blood, not unto judgement but as a remedy.

THE DIGNITY OF THE LAITY

#32 *There is, therefore, one chosen people of God: 'one Lord, one faith, one baptism' (Eph. 4:5); there is a common dignity of members deriving from their rebirth in Christ, a common grace as sons, a common vocation to perfection, one salvation, one hope and undivided charity.*

Clement of Alexandria, in the *Paidagogos*, gives us a great sense both of the uniqueness and the solidarity of the members of the early Church:

> 1.6.38[8] ... He says in the Gospel of John, 'Eat my flesh and drink my blood (Jn. 6:53). Here He uses food and drink as a striking figure for faith and for the promise. Through

[6]Text: CSEL 34.655   [7]Text: PL 39.1975   [8]Text: SC 70.180

these, the Church, composed of many members as man is, receives nourishment and growth; she is welded together and formed into a unit out of body, which is faith, and soul, which is hope, just as the Lord is fashioned from flesh and blood. Hope, indeed, which holds faith together as its soul, is the blood of faith. Once hope is extinguished, then the life-principle of faith expires, as when blood is drawn from the veins.

And, in the same work, speaking of the over-arching importance of charity, he says:

2.1.5[9] An Agape is in reality heavenly food, a banquet of the Word. The Agape, or charity 'bears all things, endures all things, hopes all things, charity never fails' (1 Cor. 13:7) ... 6 On this charity depend the whole law and the world. If you love the Lord and your neighbor (cf. Mk. 12:30-31) there will be a feast, a heavenly one, in heaven... 'for the Kingdom of God does not consist in food and drink', that is, the daily meal, but 'justice and peace and joy in the Holy Spirit' (Rom.14:17). Whoever eats of this feast is put in possession of the most wonderful of all things, the Kingdom of God, and takes his place in the holy assembly of love, the heavenly Church.

Theodore of Mopsuestia is one of our best sources on the liturgy and theology of early baptism. He shows its ecclesial dimensions in this excerpt:

15 [10] Next in sequence in the baptismal profession they profess faith in 'one catholic church'. I am baptized in order to become a member of the great body of Christ; as the blessed Paul says, There is one body, one Spirit, just as you were all called into one same hope when you were called (Eph. 4:4). Certainly it is not just this edifice constructed by men that is called 'church', although it has received the name because of the union of the faithful that

[9]Text: SC 108.18   [10]Text: *Studi e Testi*, 141

has taken place. The name 'church' is applied to the total
assembly of the faithful who serve God in an orthodox
fashion, those who, since the coming of Christ have
believed in Him in every place until the consummation of
the world and the coming of our Saviour which we await
from Heaven, because our Saviour Himself said to his
blessed apostles, 'Go, teach all nations and baptize them
in the name of the Father, Son and Holy Spirit, teaching
them to keep my commandments', and adds, 'I will be
with you all days, even to the consummation of the world'
(Mt. 28:19-20).

APOSTOLATE OF THE LAITY

#33 *All the laity, then, have the exalted duty of working for
the ever greater spread of the divine plan of salvation to all
men, of every epoch and all over the earth.*

John Chrysostom powerfully evokes the parable of the
leaven to show the potential of the laity for the spread of the
Gospel[11]:

> For as the leaven converts the large quantity of meal into
> its own quality (cf. Mt. 13:33) even so shall you convert the
> whole world...Let nobody reprove us, therefore, for
> being few. For great is the power of the Gospel and what
> is once leavened becomes leaven in turn for the remain-
> der...Now if twelve men leavened the whole world,
> imagine the extent of our weakness in that we cannot, in
> spite of our numbers, improve what is left. We who ought
> to be enough for ten thousand worlds and to become
> leaven to them. 'But', you object, 'they were apostles'. So
> what! Were they not partakers with you? Were they not
> raised in cities? Did they not enjoy the same benefits? Did
> they not practice trades? What, were they angels? Did
> they come down from Heaven? (in Matt.46[47],2).

[11] Text: PG 58.478

We know of the active collaboration of laity with clergy from a letter like the following from the Roman church to Cyprian:

> ep. XXX[12] What you have also yourself declared in so important a matter meets our approval, that the peace of the Church be a top priority. Then, that a consultative assembly be gathered together, consisting of bishops, presbyters, deacons and confessors, as well as of laity, who are steadfast and deal with the case of the lapsed.

[The laity] are gathered together in the People of God and established in the Body of Christ under one Head.

St. John Chrysostom, in *Homily 18 on II Corinthians*[13], says that there are times when there is no difference at all between the priest and his subjects, e.g. in partaking of the mysteries where all alike are deemed equally worthy, unlike under the Old Testament where priest and people consumed different offerings. Not so under the New. Before everybody is set out one body and one cup. They are all equal in the common prayers in Church, where the laity make their own contribution, for example, prayers for the possessed, for penitents etc... Even in the liturgy of the Eucharist, as distinct from the liturgy of the Word, priest prays for people, and people for priest in such exchanges as *The Lord be with you and also with you.* Sacred hymns, like prayers, are also shared by both. Chrysostom's reasons for going into such detail, he tells us, is so that the laity may see that they are all one body, differentiated from one another as members of a body are, and so that they may not throw the whole burden on the priests but must realize that each should contribute to the care of the Church as to a body common to all.

In *Homily 30 on I Corinthians*[14] Chrysostom goes into further detail in exegeting chapter 12 of 1 Cor., which deals

---

[12]Text: CSEL 111,2,553   [13]Text: PG 61.527   [14]Text: PG 61.249-258

with the diversity of the members (*if the whole body were an eye, where would be the hearing?*) to the conclusion: *and now there are many members but one body*) with his own concluding reflection that every single member has both a proper and a common function. He details such proper functions for all-virgins, widows, donors of alms, even beggars:

> What is lower than those who beg? And yet even these fulfill a most important function in the Church, clinging as they do to the doors of the sanctuary and supplying one of its greatest ornaments. For without these there could be no perfecting the fullness of the Church.

THE PRIESTLY OFFICE OF THE LAITY

#34 *Since he wishes to continue his witness and his service through the laity also, he gives them a share in his priestly office.*

The priesthood of the laity is invoked by Origen as a reason for exempting Christians from military service. In *Against Celsus* he writes:

> VIII.73[15] To those enemies of our faith who require us to bear arms for the common good and to kill we can reply: Do not those who are priests at certain shrines...keep their hands free from blood?

He establishes a parallel, not just between pagan and Christian priests, but between pagan priests and the entire Christian faithful, and concludes:

> VIII 73. None better than Christians fight for the Emperor, but we fight 'forming a special army' — an army of piety, by offering our prayers to God.

[15] Text: SC 150,344,346

Elsewhere, in his *Homilies on Leviticus,* Origen says:

> 9.1[16] Do you not know that the priesthood has been given to you, that is to say, to the whole church of God and to the people believers? Hear Peter say to the faithful: *a chosen race, a royal priesthood a holy nation, an acquired people.* (1 Pet. 2:9). You, then, have the priesthood since you are a priestly race, and so *you ought to offer to God a sacrifice of praise,* (cf. Heb. 13:15), a sacrifice of prayers, a sacrifice of mercy, a sacrifice of purity, a sacrifice of sanctity.

Tertullian is equally explicit concerning the priesthood of the laity:

> [17]It would be idle for us to suppose (in the case of second marriage) that what is forbidden to priests is allowed to the laity. Are not laymen also priests? The Scripture says: *He has made us a kingdom and has made us priests for God and for His Father* (Apoc.1:6)

THE PROPHETIC OFFICE

#35 *Christ is the great prophet... Until the full manifestation of his glory, he fulfills this prophetic office, not only by the hierarchy...but also by the laity...*

The *Didascalia Apostolorum* instructs the laity:

> XI[18] Be you then, O laymen, peaceable one with another, and strive like wise doves to fill the Church, and to convert and tame those that are wild, and bring them into her midst. And this is the great reward that is promised by God, if you deliver them from fire and present them to the Church firmly established and faithful.

[16]Text: SC 287.72   [17]Text: CCL 2.1024

[18]Text: ed. R.H. Connolly, 119

KINGLY ROLE OF THE LAITY

#36 *The Lord also desires that his kingdom be spread by the lay faithful: the kingdom of truth and life, the kingdom of holiness and grace, the kingdom of justice, love and peace.*

In that Christ is King of the universe (cf.1 Cor. 15:27) the laity have a special role in spreading His Kingdom. St. Basil says in *On Judgment*[19]:

> Neglect of the one true and only King of all leads to great strife and dissension among churchmen, each deserting the teaching of Christ, and arbitrarily appropriating to himself teachings and definitions.... Disagreeements among us are a sign that we have either deserted or denied our future King.

John Chrysostom, In *Homily 3.7 on II Corinthians*[20] links the laity's participation in the triple role of priest, prophet and king to the reception of baptism:

> In baptism you have become king, and priest, and prophet: a king, in that you have dashed to earth all the deeds of wickedness and slain your sins; a priest, in that you offer yourself to God, having sacrificed your body and being yourself slain also, 'for if we died with Him we shall also live with Him, (2 Tim. 2:11); a prophet, knowing what shall be, and being inspired of God, and sealed. For as upon soldiers a seal is imprinted, so upon the faithful the seal of the Spirit is also imprinted.

THE LAITY AND THE HIERARCHY

#37 *By reason of the knowledge, competence or pre-eminence which they have, the laity are empowered — indeed sometimes obliged — to manifest their opinion on those things which pertain to the good of the Church.*

[19]Text: PG 31.656   [20]Text: PG 61.417

#38 *Each individual layman must be a witness before the world to the resurrection and life of the Lord Jesus, and a sign of the living God. All together, and each one to the best of his ability, must nourish the world with spiritual fruits (cf. Gal. 5:22). They must diffuse in the world the spirit which animates those poor, meek and peace-makers whom the Lord in the Gospel proclaimed blessed (cf. Mt. 5:3-9). In a word: 'what the soul is in the body, let Christians be in the world.*

SUMMARY
The concluding paragraph on The Laity ends with an explicit quotation from *The Epistle to Diognetus*. The chapter deserves to be quoted here in full. Diognetus was an influential pagan and lived perhaps in the middle of the second century, and the author belongs to the group of writers called the Greek Apologists:

> 6 [21] In a word, what the soul is to the body Christians are to the world. The soul is distributed in every member of the body, and Christians are scattered in every city in the world. The soul dwells in the body, and yet it is not of the body. So, Christians live in the world but they are not of the world. The soul which is guarded in the visible body is not itself visible. Likewise, Christians who are in the world are known, but their worship remains unseen. The flesh hates the soul and acts like an unjust aggressor, because it is forbidden to indulge in pleasures. The world hates Christians, not that they have done it wrong but because they oppose its pleasures. The soul loves the body and its members in spite of the hatred. So Christians love those who hate them. The soul is imprisoned in the body yet it holds the body together. Likewise Christians are imprisoned in the world, yet it is they who hold the world together. The immortal soul dwells in a mortal tabernacle. Likewise Christians sojourn amid perishable things but their souls are set on immortality in heaven. When the soul is frustrated in the matter of food and

[21]Text: SC 33.

drink it is improved. Likewise when Christians are perse-
cuted they increase numerically every day. This is the
assignment to which God has summoned them and they
are not free to decline.

Finally, this paragraph speaks of the laity having an
obligation to diffuse in the world the spirit which animates
the poor, and the meek, the peacemakers proclaimed
blessed in the beatitudes (Mt. 5:3-9). As an example of one
Father's attempt to raise the level of social conscience in his
congregation we will again cite John Chrysostom, from his
Homilies on Matthew:

> h.66 [22] By now I am ashamed to speak of almsgiving.
> Having frequently spoken on the topic my results show
> little relation to my efforts. There has been some rise in
> contributions, but not what I would have wished. I see
> you sowing but not with a generous hand. So my fear is
> that you will also reap sparingly (cf. 2 Cor. 11:6). To
> prove that we sow sparingly just ask ourselves what class
> is in the majority in this city (Antioch) — rich or poor? Or
> whether the middle income group is in the majority? For
> instance, ten per cent are rich, ten per cent are poor, the
> have-nots, and the rest are middle income. So distribute
> the poor among the rest of the population and you will
> see proportions of the social disgrace. The super-rich are
> indeed very few, but the next income group is very
> numerous, and the poor are proportionately much fewer.
> Nevertheless, although those who could feed the hungry
> are very numerous, many go to sleep hungry, because of
> the barbarity and inhumanity of those who could easily
> come to their rescue. For if both the wealthy and the
> middle income people were to distribute among them-
> selves those in need of food and clothing, the distribution
> would only be about one poor person to fifty less poor, or
> even a hundred. Yet the complaints of the poor are heard
> daily in the midst of so many who are well-off.

[22]Text: PG 58.630; cf. NPNF 10.407

Chrysostom feels that the Church is setting a pretty good example in alleviating the needs of the poor:

> So that you may grasp the extent of the inhumanity of others recall that church revenues are at best upper middle class, certainly not wealthy, and yet consider the number of widows it helps every day, the number of virgins; the list of those receiving church aid already exceeds three thousand.
>
> As well as these, the church helps those in prison, in hospitals, those away from home, the handicapped, the altar attendants, and the casual callers for food and clothing on a day-to-day basis. And yet the Church does not exhaust its resources. So, if only ten men were willing to spend in similar fashion, the problem of poverty would be eliminated.
>
> But what, you will ask, will we have left to will to our children? The principal will be intact, and the interest will increase, stored up for them in Heaven. Are you not willing to do this? At least, do half of it, at least a third part, at least a tenth. Thanks to God's goodness one city could take care of the poor of ten cities.

V

The Call to Holiness

THE HOLINESS OF THE CHURCH

#39 *Therefore all in the Church, whether they belong to the hierarchy or are cared for by it, are called to holiness, according to the apostle's saying: 'For this is the will of God, your sanctification' (1 Thess. 4:3).*

The patristic call to holiness, or perfection, is extended to all, with little or no distinction made between lay and cleric. All Christians are followers of Christ and, as Gregory of Nyssa said in his *On Perfection*, 'it is necessary to show through our life that we ourselves are what the power of this great name requires us to be.' In fact, Gregory's subtitle of his work is 'On What it is Necessary for a Christian to be'. For Gregory three things characterize the life of Christ: action, word and thought. Christian perfection consists in the participation of one's soul, speech and activities in all of the names by which Christ is signified (Gregory analyses thirty such names in the course of his treatise, e.g. Power of God, Peace, Passover, Propitiation) so that perfect holiness, according to Paul's eulogy, is taken upon oneself 'in the whole body, and soul, and spirit (1 Thess. 5:23), continuously safeguarding against being confused with evil'.

Likewise, in a companion work called *On What it means to Call Oneself a Christian*, Gregory of Nyssa says[1]:

[1] Text: PG 46.244

It is not possible for Christ not to be justice, purity, truth, and estrangement from all evil, nor is it possible to be a Christian, that is, truly a Christian, without displaying in oneself a participation in these virtues. If one might give a definition of Christianity we shall define it as follows: Christianity is an imitation (*mimesis*) of the divine nature.

St. Augustine, in his *Of True Religion*, clearly delineates the role of the Catholic Church in the pursuit of sanctity and the diverse paths by which all human beings may come eventually to grace and truth:

5.9[2] Religion is to be sought neither in the confusion of the pagans, nor in the offscourings of the heretics, nor in the insipidity of the schismatics, nor in the blindness of the Jews, but only among those who are called Catholic or orthodox Christians, that is, guardians of truth and followers of right.

6.10 This Catholic Church, strongly and widely spread throughout the world, makes use of all who err, to correct them if they are willing to be aroused, and to assist its own progress. It makes use of the pagans as material for its operations, of heretics to test its own doctrine, of schismatics to prove its stability, of the Jews as a foil for its own beauty. Some it invites, others it excludes, some it leaves behind, others it leads. To all it gives power to participate in the grace of God, whether they have yet to be formed, or are in need of reform, admitted for the first time, or re-admitted.

Its own dissolute members, that is, those whose lives or opinions are dissolute, it tolerates like the chaff which protects the corn on the threshing-floor until it is separated from its awnings. On this floor everyone freely makes himself either corn or chaff. Therefore every man's sin or error is tolerated until he finds an accuser, or defends his erroneous opinion with unyielding animosity. Those who are excommunicated return by way of peni-

[2]Text: CCL 32.194

tence, or they are free to sink into wickedness as a warning to us to be vigilant, or they cause schisms to exercise our patience, or they produce a heresy to test our intelligence, or to sharpen it.

Perhaps no Father more than St. Augustine dealt with the problem of the place of sinners in a Church one of whose distinguishing marks was holiness. As he dealt with the Donatist heresy, and also with the Pelagian, various facets of his thought emerged. For the Donatists the church was so holy that there was no room in her for sinners. For the Pelagians holiness was largely a matter of human effort and merit; there was no original sin, and consequently no need for redemption. Augustine has a double vision of the Church, the church now, which of necessity is less than perfect, and the church in the resurrection of the dead which will contain the truly elect. He explains part of his vision of the nature of church in a homily on the two catches of fish in the New Testament:

> h.248[3] Today the reading taken from the Gospel (Jn. 21: 1-14) was taken from the Evangelist John and concerned events which occurred after our Lord's resurrection. You and I heard that the Lord Jesus Christ showed Himself to His disciples at the sea of Tiberias; He who had already made them fishers of men found them still fishers of fish. Throughout the whole night they had taken nothing, but when they saw the Lord and at His behest let down the nets, they caught the large number you have heard mentioned (i.e. 153). . . . Why, therefore, could it be of interest to Jesus Christ if fishes were caught or not? Now this fishing episode is a clue. Let me recall with you the two hauls of fish made by the apostles at the directions of our Lord Jesus Christ. One was before the Passion (cf. Lk. 5: 4-11), the other after the Resurrection. In these two catches of fish, therefore, the whole Church is represented, both as she is now, and as she will be in the resurrection of the dead. For now she has multitudes

[3]Text: PL 38.1158

without numbers, both good and bad; after the Resurrection, however, she will have only the good in a fixed number.

ALL CHRISTIANS CALLED TO HOLINESS

#40 *In order to reach this perfection the faithful should use the strength dealt out to them by Christ's gift, so that, following in his footsteps and conformed to his image, doing the will of God in everything, they may wholeheartedly devote themselves to the glory of God and to the service of their neighbor.*

The idea of perfection is familiar in the *Didache*:[4]

'If anyone strikes you on the right cheek, turn the other to him' and you will be perfect (1.4), and: If you are able to carry the full yoke of the Law you will be perfect (6.2).

In a mysterious phrase Ignatius of Antioch tells the Ephesians:

He who has made the words of Jesus really his own is able also to hear his silence. Thus he will be perfect; he will act through his speech and be known by his silence.' (15.2, SC 10.70).

Origen further defines the notion in his *Commentary on Romans*[5]:

7.7. The verse says: 'To those that love God all things collaborate unto good'. The Christian must conform himself to the image of Christ; the Christian becomes Christ's spirit when he has so attached himself to the Word and Wisdom of God in all things that in no way is the image and likeness discolored. And thus if one wishes to attain to the summit of perfection and beatitude one seeks after the likeness of Christ's image, the image of the son of God.

4Text: SC 248.144,168   5Text: PG 14.1124

In ps.-Macarius *On Prayer*, c.XI (PG 34.861) we are told that 'perfection, which means complete and absolute purity from evil affections through sharing in the good Spirit, is enjoined by God on all'.

Already in Clement of Rome, in a paraphrase of Paul's chapter on the primacy of love (1 Cor. 13), we read:

> 49[6] Love creates no schism, love does not quarrel, love preserves perfect harmony. In love all the elect of God have been rendered perfect. Without love nothing is pleasing to God.

UNITY AND DIVERSITY OF HOLINESS

#41 *The forms and tasks of life are many but holiness is one... Each one, however, according to his own gifts and duties must steadfastly advance along the way of a living faith, which arouses hope and works through love.*

John Chrysostom, for all his negative reputation as a misogynist, has some fairly positive things to say about marriage, for instance in *Homily 20 on the Epistle to the Ephesians*:

> 20.2[7] Hence Christ said, "He who made them from the beginning made them male and female" (Mt. 19:4). From this source great evils are produced, and great blessings, both to families and to states. There is nothing which so welds our life together as the love of man and wife. For this many will lay aside their arms, many will give up life itself. And Paul would never, without some reason and object, have gone to such trouble on this subject, for instance when he says, "Wives, be subject to your husbands, as to the Lord" (Eph. 5:22). Why so? Because when they live in harmony, the children are well brought up, and the servants are orderly, and neighbors, friends and relations enjoy the fragrance. But if it is otherwise

[6]Text: SC 167.180   [7]Text: PG62.135

everything is topsy turvy and in disarray. Just as when the generals of an army are at peace among themselves everything else is in proper order but if they are at variance everything else is in disarray, so, I say, it is with marriage. That is why he said, "Wives, be subject to your husbands as to the Lord".

Elsewhere, in his *Homilies on Matthew*, Chrysostom writes:

7 [8] I do not prohibit marriage, or prevent your taking pleasure in it, but I would wish it to be done with chastity, not with wantonness, and reproach, and endless recriminations. I do not lay it down as a law that you are to occupy the mountains and deserts, but I command you to be good, considerate and chaste, though dwelling in the heart of the city. For, in fact, all our laws are common to the monks also, except marriage.

CHARITY, THE FIRST AND MOST NECESSARY GIFT

#42 *God has poured out his love in our hearts through the Holy Spirit who has been given to us; therefore the first and most necessary gift is charity, by which we love God above all things and our neighbor because of him.*

Dorotheus of Gaza, in his treatise *On Renunciation*, says[9]:

The ten commandments were given to all Christians and it is understood that every Christian observes them: this is, as it were, the tribute appointed to be paid by the King.... There are, however, in the world great and illustrious men who not only pay him the appointed tribute but also offer gifts... These gifts are virginity and poverty. These are not commanded but freely given.

[8] Text: PG 57.81

[9] Text: PG 88.1629; tr. E.P. Wheeler, *Dorotheos of Gaza, Discourses and Sayings*, Kalamazoo, 1977, 84.

Nowhere is it written, you shall not take a wife or beget children. Neither did Christ give the commandment, 'Sell your property'. When the lawyer approached him... He replied, 'you know the commandments, Do not kill' etc... He added, 'if you want to be perfect, sell your property....'

The Means of Holiness

Towering among these counsels is that precious gift of divine grace given to some by the Father to devote themselves to God alone more easily with an undivided heart in virginity or celibacy.

There is no shortage of materials on virginity or celibacy among the Fathers. Tertullian wrote a treatise called *Exhortation to Chastity*, and even when he, a married man addressed himself explicitly to the subject of marriage he seldom gives it more than a second-class status. Gregory of Nyssa and John Chrysostom each wrote major treatises *On Virginity*, as did Basil of Ancyra, and there is one ascribed to Athanasius. Cyprian speaks for them all when he describes virgins, in *On the Dress of Virgins*,

> 3[10] They are the flower of the tree that is the Church, the beauty and adornment of spiritual grace...the image of God reflecting the holiness of the Lord, the more illustrious part of Christ's flock. The glorious fruitfulness of Mother Church rejoices through them.

Basil of Ancyra says:

> 2[11] Virginity is a great blessing, indeed, making man in supreme measure most like to the incorruptible God.

St. Cyprian, in addressing rich women who displayed their riches and felt that they ought to use the blessings that

---

[10] Text: CSEL 111,1,189   [11] Text: PG 30.672.

they owned, stresses that only she is truly rich who is rich in God and truly wealthy who is wealthy in Christ, and that the only true blessings are spiritual ones which lead us to God and remain with us in everlasting possession with God:

> 7 [12] Eternal and divine things therefore must be sought, and all things must be done in accordance with the will of God, that we may follow the footsteps and instructions of our Lord who has warned us and said: 'I have not come down from Heaven to do my own will, but the will of Him who sent me' (Jn.6:38). But if the servant is not greater than the master, and the freedman owes allegiance to his deliverer, we who desire to be Christians ought to imitate the words of Christ. It has been written, and read, and heard, and has been proclaimed for our instruction through the mouth of the Church: 'He that says that he abides in Christ ought himself walk in the footsteps of Christ (1 Jn.2:6). We must keep in step with Him. We must strive to imitate His pace. Then our striving for truth shall be in step with our faith in His name, and the believer is rewarded if he puts into practice what he believes.

Martyrdom: Supreme Testimony of Love

The possibility of martyrdom is lightly touched on at this point in *Lumen Gentium* but it is well to remember that it was a day-to-day reality for lengthy periods in early Christianity. Theodoret of Cyrus, in his *Curatio* gives us a bird's eye view of history to his own day:

> IX.20[13] Neither Caligula nor Claudius were able to destroy the laws of the fishermen, the publicans and the tent-maker. Nero, who succeeded them, was no more successful despite his attack on our legislators (for he actually killed Peter and Paul but in killing them he failed to surpress their laws). Vespasian, Titus, and Domitian

[12]Text: CSEL 111,1,193   [13]Text: SC 57.342

were equally unsuccessful. Domitian used every strata-
gem against them. You know how many he condemned
to death and with what a variety of torments. Trajan and
Hadrian both waged violent campaigns against these
laws. Trajan indeed destroyed the Persian dynasty and
brought the Armenians under Roman sway; he com-
pelled the Scythians to bow to Roman rule but had no
power to destroy the legislation of the fishermen and the
tent-maker. Hadrian annihilated the city of those who
had crucified Jesus, but he failed to persuade Christian
believers to quit Christ's service.... Not to mention
Commodus, Maximian and all the emperors up to Aure-
lian, Carus and Carinus, who does not know of the
anti-religious furor of a Diocletian, a Maximian, a Max-
ence, a Maximinus and a Licinius? It was not just singly,
or in twos, or threes, that they killed the Christian believers, but in crowds, by the thousands, and tens of
thousands.

VI

Religious

THE EVANGELICAL COUNSELS

#43 *The teaching and example of Christ provide the foundation for the evangelical counsels of chaste self-dedication to God, of poverty and of obedience.*

The (evangelical) counsels are a divine gift, which the Church has received from her Lord and which she ever preserves with the help of His grace.

Origen clearly distinguishes, in his *Commentary on Matthew*, between what is a matter of precept and what a matter of counsel:

> 15.16[1] Precepts are given to pay debts. But what we do over and above what we owe we do not do by precept. For instance, virginity is not a payment of a debt, nor is it demanded by a precept, but it is offered over and above what is owed.

And Cyprian, in his *Dress of Virgins*, counsels:

> 11[2] You say that you are wealthy and rich...Use your riches but for your salvation and for your good works ... Let the poor feel that you are rich; let the needy feel

---

[1]Text: PG 13.1300   [2]Text: PL 4.449

that you are wealthy. Through your patrimony make God your debtor. Feed Christ.

Tertullian, in his *Exhortation to Chastity*, says:

10[3] Continence will be a means to deal in the mighty substance of sanctity. By parsimony of the flesh you will gain the Spirit.

A deep ascetical vein runs through the writings of Tertullian which radically affected the history of the Church. Here we give three representative texts, from the *Apology, To His Wife* and *On the Spectacles*.

9,18[4] Then, further, wherever you (i.e. non-Christians) are — at home, away from home, overseas — your lust is always in attendance. Its wholesale indulgence, or even its indulgence on a limited scale, may easily and unintentionally beget children anywhere, so that in this way a progeny scattered around in the business of life may have intercourse with their own kith and kin without ever suspecting that they may be guilty of incest. We, however, have been safeguarded from this by a persevering and steadfast chastity. We abstain from adultery of any sort and any post-matrimonial infidelity, and so we are saved from any incestuous consequences. Some of us, making matters doubly secure, completely repel the power of sensual sin by virginal continence, so that boyish sinlessness is preserved into old age. If you would only realize that the sins I have mentioned are widespread among you, then you would conclude that they have no place among Christians. Both facts would be obvious to the same examination. But blindness to both facts is more likely to be the prevailing attitude, so that those who do not see what is there are apt to imagine what is not. (*Apology*)

[3]Text: CCL 2.1029   [4]Text: CCL 1.104

6[5]...she whose husband is deceased should henceforth abstain from sex by not re-marrying, an abstinence which numerous pagan women devote to the memory of beloved husbands. When something seems difficult we should compare with others who have to cope with greater difficulties. How many are they who from the first moment of their baptism seal their flesh with the seal of virginity? Furthermore, how many by equal, mutual consent cancel the marriage debt, becoming voluntary eunuchs in their desire for the celestial kingdom? Now if abstinence can be endured while the marriage bond is still intact how much more so when it is at an end? For I think it is more difficult to forsake completely what is still intact than to cease yearning for what is no longer there. Hard and arduous, doubtless, is continence for God's sake of a holy woman after her husband has died, while pagans, in honor of their Satan, can undertake priestly offices which involve both virginity and widowhood! (*To His Wife*)

29[6] For what more delightful than to have God the Father and our Lord at peace with us, than revelation of the truth, than confession of our errors, than pardon of the countless sins of our past life? What greater pleasure than distaste of pleasure itself, contempt of everything the world can offer us, true liberty, a pure conscience, a contented wife, and freedom from all fear of death? What nobler than to tread underfoot the gods of the gentiles, to exorcise evil spirits, to perform cures, to seek divine revelations, to live for God? These are the pleasures, these the spectacles that befit Christians — holy, everlasting, free. Reckon these as your circus games, fix your eyes on the circuits of the world, the revolving seasons; reckon up the periods of time; long for the goal of the final consummation, defend the societies of the churches, be startled at the sound of God's signal, be aroused at the angel's trumpet, glory in the prize of martyrdom. If you take pleasure in the literature of drama we have our own

[5]Text: CCL 1.380   [6]Text: CCL 1.251

literature in abundance. Plenty of verse, sententious literature, songs, proverbs. And these are not fictitious, but true; not rhetorical tricks but plain realities. Would you also like fights and wrestling contests? Well, there is no shortage of these, and they are not without significance. Watch unchastity being overcome by chastity, perfidy being slain by fidelity, cruelty smitten by compassion, impurity being upstaged by modesty. These are our contests; it is in these that we win our crowns. Do you also wish for some blood? You have Christ's. (*On the Spectacles*)

Lactantius, in his *Divine Institutes*, takes up the evangelical counsel of chastity after his discussion of Christian marriage:

6.23[7]...Furthermore, not only adultery must be avoided, but even the very consideration of it, lest anyone look upon another woman and desire her in his heart.... Even though the body be contaminated with no stain, the condition of purity does not exist, however, if the soul is defiled; nor can chastity seem unblemished where desire has marred the conscience.

In truth, no one should consider it difficult to impose a bridle on pleasure and to enclose a roaming, wandering spirit, so to speak, within the bounds of chastity and purity, since it has been proposed to man to conquer it, and since very many have retained a blessed, uncorrupted integrity of body, and since there are many who now enjoy most happily this heavenly kind of life. But God does not command that this be done by way of precept, since there must be place for human generation, but rather by way of counsel. He Himself knows how powerful He has made the emotions. 'If anyone can do this,'He says, 'he will have an exceeding, incomparable reward'. This sort of continence is, so to speak, the peak and consummation of all the virtues, If anyone can lean

[7]Text: CSEL 19.570

toward this and strive after it, the Lord will own him as His servant; the Master will recognize this man as His disciple. Such a man will triumph over the earth.

Jerome paints a non-idealized portrait of the trials endured by him as a monk still bothered with the temptations of the world, flesh and devil.

ep.22.7[8] How often when I was established in the desert and in that vast solitude which is scorched by the sun's heat and provides a rude habitation for monks, used I imagine I was back amid the pleasures of Rome! I would sit alone, filled as I was with bitterness. My limbs were ' roughly clad in sackcloth — an unseemly sight. My neglected skin resembled the body of an Ethiopian. I wept and groaned every day, and whenever I was overcome by sleep despite my resistance, I bruised my recalcitrant bones upon the bare earth. Of food and drink I say nothing, since even the sick drink only cold water, and cooked food is a luxury. So there I was, I who had condemned myself to a prison like that because of my fear of hell, with nothing but scorpions and wild beasts to keep me company. Yet I was often surrounded by dancing girls. My face was pale from fasting but my mind was inflamed with desire in a body cold as ice. Though my flesh, before its occupant, was already virtually dead, the fire of the passions kept boiling within me.

And so, destitute of help, I used to lie at the feet of Jesus, and bathe them with my tears and wipe them with my hair (cf. Lk. 7:44). When my flesh rebelled I would subdue it by weeks of fasting. I do not blush at my unfortunate state, indeed I lament that I am no longer as I was then. I remember that I often joined day to night with my lamentations and only ceased beating my breast when peace of mind returned with the Lord's rebuke. I was even afraid of my little cell — as though it was aware of my thoughts. Angry at myself and tense, I used to go out alone into the desert. Whenever I saw a deep valley, or a

[8]Text: CSEL 54.152

rugged mountain, or a jutting crag, I made it my place of prayer, my place of punishment for my wretched flesh.

Jerome derives mystical significance for the religious life from a contemplation of Jacob's ladder (cf. Gen.28:12). He imagines that it has fifteen rungs. As director of monks he daily preached his *Homilies on the Psalms* from which this is taken:

> 41[9] Jacob saw there a ladder set up on the ground with its top reaching to heaven; and in Heaven the Lord leaning on it. And he saw angels ascending and descending. He saw angels ascending — holy men going from earth to heaven; he saw angels descending — the devil and his whole army cast down from heaven. It is very difficult to ascend from earth to heaven. We fall more easily than we rise. We fall easily; it requires great labor, a great deal of sweat to climb upwards. If I am on the lowest step, how many more are there before I reach heaven? If I am on the second, the third, the fourth, the tenth, what benefit to me unless I arrive at the top? Grant with me that this ladder has fifteen rungs. I climb as high as the fourteenth, but unless I reach and stay on the fifteenth, what profit to me to have climbed the fourteenth? Should I fall after arriving at the fifteenth, the higher the climb, the greater the fall.
>
> Now meditate on the mystical significance of the ladder. It requires great pain, severe effort, to climb from earth to heaven. Would you like to know what are the steps? What is the first one? Fasting is the first one, in my opinion, for we are still quite close to the earth. We are withdrawing from the earth, beginning to climb. Nevertheless our mind is still on material things; we are still preoccupied with concern for the body.... Abstinence is the first step. Do not jump to the conclusion, however, that if you fast you will ascend all at once to the kingdom of heaven. Fasts do not necessarily lead to the kingdom of heaven, but without them we shall not arrive there. Fasts

[9]Text: CCL 78.248; cf. FOTC 48.302

by themselves are worthless; with other things they help. Fasting is, so to speak, the foundation and support of those who are mounting to greater heights.

The second step is true renouncement of the world. It consists in aiming at nothing of this world, in despising everything earthly. Detachment, then, you may ask, is the second step? Yes, the second. it is nothing, however, to give up the things of the world; to renounce vice, that is the noble thing. If I should fast, if I am on the first step; if I should give away all my possessions, if I am on the second step, what does it profit me if I am quarrelsome, if I give vent to my anger, if I criticize and slander, if I am envious?

Renouncing the world is nothing great; there are greater things that must be rejected. Someone may interpose: But that is difficult, severe, hard. But that is exactly what makes it great — its difficulty. Christ's athlete is only crowned if he enters the contest and competes according to the rules. Do not give up hope though the climb is arduous and difficult and begets despair. Do not lose confidence, man. The Lord is up there on the fifteenth step. He is watching over you. He is helping you. If you are only on the first step and the passage from the first to the fifteenth seems impossible, do not look back at the steps; look up at the Lord. Attend to what Scripture says. . . Jacob saw Him leaning over the ladder (cf. Gen. 28:13). Realize what that means. From where He was standing He stooped down and lowered Himself that we might ascend. The Lord stooped down; He humbled Himself for your sake. Ascend, therefore, with safety and confidence.

THE RELIGIOUS STATE: NATURE AND IMPORTANCE

#44 *The religious state constitutes a closer imitation and an abiding reenactment in the Church of the form of life which the Son of God made his own when he came into the world*

to do the will of the Father and which he propounded to the
disciples who followed him.

A monk, in the definition of Maximus the Confessor, is
one who separates his mind from material things and by
self-mastery, charity, psalmody and prayer devotes himself
to God (*char.* 2.54). For Maximus, 'the monk's accomplish-
ments are to possess nothing, to have no reputation, to have
no influence, but self-mastery, suffering of evil, and all that
goes with these' (*char.* 3.85). In *The First Greek Life of
Pachomius* we get a good definition of a monk as a result of
Pachomius' visit to Palamon, c.316 A.D.:

> 6[10] Then, moved by the love of God, he sought to become
> a monk. When he was told of an anchorite called
> Palamon, he went to him to share his anchoritic life.
> When he arrived, he knocked on the door. The old man
> looked down from above and said, 'What do you want?'
> — for he was abrupt in speech. He replied, 'I ask you,
> father, make me a monk.' He said to him, 'You cannot.
> This work of God is not so simple; for many have come
> but have not persevered.' Pachomius said, 'Put me to the
> test at it and see'. The old man spoke again, 'First try
> yourself out for a while, then come here again. For I have
> a hard *ascesis*. In summer I fast daily and in winter I eat
> every other day. By the grace of God I eat nothing but
> bread and salt. I am not in the habit of (using) oil and
> wine. I keep vigil as I was taught, always spending half the
> night and often the whole night in prayer and reciting of
> the words of God.' When the youth heard the old man say
> this, he was still more strengthened in spirit to endure
> every hardship with him. 'I believe', he said to him, 'that
> with the help of God and your prayers, I will endure all
> that you have told me.' Then opening the door, the old
> man let him in and clothed him in the monk's habit.

[10]Text: Trans. *Pachomian Koinonia* 1, 301, Tr. A. Veilleux, Kalamazoo, MI,
1980.

There is an unforgettable portrait of early monasticism in
The Life of Saint Antony, written by Athanasius:

> 44[11] So, then, their solitary cells in the hills were like tents
> filled with divine choirs — singing Psalms, studying,
> fasting, praying, rejoicing in the hope of the life to come,
> and laboring in order to give alms, and preserving love
> and harmony among themselves. And truly it was like
> seeing a land apart, a land of piety and justice. For there
> was neither wrongdoer nor sufferer of wrong, nor was
> there reproof of the tax-collector; but a multitude of
> ascetics, all with one set purpose —virtue.

Antony died in the year 356 at the ripe age of one hundred
and five, and Athanasius may have begun writing his life the
following year, although some doubts persist about the
authenticity of the work. It is nonetheless an eloquent tribute to the father of Christian monasticism, who spent
twenty years in solitary asceticism before beginning the
movement which culminated in 'inducing many to take up
the monastic life. And so now monasteries also sprang up in
the mountains and the desert was populated with monks
who left their own people and registered themselves for
citizenship in Heaven' (*Life*, 14).

Jerome gives an extended account of the monks of Egypt
in one of his letters;

> ep. 22 34:[12] And since I have mentioned the monks, and
> know you would like to hear of holy things, bear with me
> a little. In Egypt there are three classes of monks. There
> are the cenobites, whom they call in their own dialect
> *sauhes*; we can describe them as those living in a com-
> munity. The anchorites, who live alone in the desert, are
> called by this name because they have withdrawn from
> society. The third class is what they call *remnouth*, a very
> low, despised type, the only ones of the principal kind

[11]Text: PG 26.908; Trans., ACW 10 (1950), R.T.Meyer, 57.
[12]Text: CSEL 54.196, cf. ACW 33.16

found in our province. These dwell together by twos and threes, not many more, and live according to their own wishes and independently. They contribute part of their earnings to a common fund, to ensure a common supply of food. They live for the most part in cities and fortified towns, and whatever they sell is very expensive; I presume it is their craftsmanship, not their life, that is sacred. They often fight among themselves because, being self-supporting they do not admit to being dependent on anyone. They actually compete with one another in fasting. They turn what should be done in secret into competitive triumphalism. Among them everything is done for effect. They wear loose sleeves, flapping boots, awkward clothing. They sigh a great deal, make visits to virgins, criticise the clergy, and gorge themselves on feast days.

35 So, ridding ourselves of these like the plague, let us come to the ones who live in common; that is, the ones whom we have said are called cenobites. Their first rule in community is to obey their superiors, carrying out their orders. They are subdivided into tens and hundreds, so that the tenth man is in charge of nine, and the one hundredth has ten officers under him. They live in separate but adjacent cells. Until the ninth hour there is a kind of cessation of intercourse, no one visiting his neighbor, except the aforementioned deans. This is so that anyone troubled in mind may be consoled by their conversation. After the ninth hour they convene, sing psalms, and the Scriptures are usually read. When prayers are finished all take their seats and one, whom they call their father, stands up in their midst and begins to expound. While he speaks, no one dares look at another, or cough. The audience weep to show their approval of the speaker. Tears roll silently down their cheeks, and their sorrow is manifested without even a sob. But when he begins to proclaim God's kingdom, their future blessedness, and the glory to come, you could see all sighing gently, lifting their eyes aloft and saying gently: "Who will give me wings like a dove, and I will fly and be at rest?"

After this the congregation is dispersed and they go in

groups of ten with their 'father' to the tables, which they serve in rotation for a week at a time. There is no confusion while dining; nobody speaks. They live on bread, beans, and vegetables seasoned with salt and oil. Only the older men receive wine. They often eat in the company of children so that the age of the one group may be uplifted and the youth of the other not weakened. After that they rise together and after singing a hymn return to their cells.

It is clear, however, that renunciation was not always as wholehearted as was desirable in the early Church. Jerome is merciless in his satirical portrayal of the worldly monk of his day:

Ep.125.16[13] But I myself have seen monks of quite a different stamp from this, men whose renunciation of the world has consisted merely in a change of clothes, and a mouthing of words, while their real life and their former habits have remained unchanged. Their belongings have increased rather than diminished. They still have the same servants and keep the same table. Out of cheap glasses and common terracotta they swallow gold. Surrounded by swarms of servants they claim for themselves the name of hermits.

Others who, though poor, think of themselves as different, walk in solemn procession through the streets, and do nothing but snarl at everyone they meet. Others shrug their shoulders and croak out what is best known to themselves. With eyes fixed on the ground they balance swollen words on their lips. Only a towncrier is missing to persuade you that it is His Excellency, the Prefect, who is passing.

There are also some who from the dampness of their cells and the severity of their fasts, from their weariness of solitude and from excessive study, have a buzzing in their ears all day and night, with the result that their manic

[13]Text: CSEL 56.134

melancholy needs the fomentations of Hippocrates, not just exhortations from me.

Great numbers are unable to break free from the crafts and trades which they previously engaged in. They no longer call themselves merchants, but they carry on their previous business; seeking for themselves not just 'food and clothing' as the Apostle directs (cf. Lk. 12:22), but financial profits, even greater ones than are sought for by worldly men. In earlier days the greed of sellers was kept within bounds by the action of the Aediles, or as the Greeks called them 'market inspectors', so that men could not cheat with impunity. But now persons in the religious profession are not ashamed to seek unjust profits, and the good name of Christianity is more often a cloak for fraud than a victim of it.

Paschasius of Dumium in the Iberian Peninsula, translating the *Sayings of the Desert Fathers*[14] from Greek into Latin, leaves us a cameo study of a monk who is the antithesis of this worldliness:

> Abbot Agatho was quite careless with those who wanted to buy his handicraft — the price of sieves was 100 nummi, and of baskets 250. He would mention the price to customers, but would accept whatever they offered without even counting it. For he would say: 'What good does it do me to quarrel with them, perhaps making them perjure themselves as well as their act of fraud. Since I have enough why should I demand money from my brothers?... When the brother said, Where are you going to get bread for your cell? he answered, 'What is the bread of a man in a cell?'

Macarius the Great in his *Spiritual Homilies* describes very well the foundations of mutual charity on which a truly Christian monastic center must be built:

[14]Text: PG 65.108

H. 3[15] The brethren ought to dwell together in much charity, whether they are praying, or reading the scriptures, or doing some kind of work, that they may have the foundation of mutual charity. In this way, those various inclinations may find favor, and those who pray, and those who read, and those who work can all live in sincerity and simplicity with one another in mutual profit. What is written? *Thy will be done on earth as in heaven.*, in order that as the angels dwell together in heaven in great concord, peace and charity, and there is no such thing there as pride, or envy, but they live together in charity and sincerity, so should the brethren dwell together. Some thirty, perhaps, are under the one rule: they cannot continue all day and night at the same thing. Some give themselves up to prayer for six hours and then would like to read; others are very willing to serve, while others work at some form of manual labor. 11. Whatever they are engaged at, the brethren ought to be in cheerfulness and charity toward one another. Let him who is at work say of him who is at prayer, 'The treasure that my brother obtains is in common, and therefore it is mine too'. Let the one who prays say of the one who reads, 'The profit which he gets from reading is to my advantage'. Let him who is at work say, 'The service which I am performing is to the advantage of all'. As the members of the body, being many, are one body '(1 Cor. 12:12), and help each other, and each performs its own function...so let the brethren be with one another.

RELIGIOUS AND THE HIERARCHY

#45 *It is for the hierarchy to make wise laws for the regulation of the practice of the counsels whereby the perfect love of God and of our neighbor is fostered in a unique way.*

Athanasius has been accused of special pleading in his account, in *The Life of Antony*, of the good relations that

[15]Text: PG 34.468

obtained between the monk, Antony, and the Church's ministers:

> 67[16] Renowned man that he was, he yet showed the profoundest respect for the Church's ministry and he wanted every cleric to be honored above himself. He was not ashamed to bow his head before bishops and priests; and if ever a deacon came to him for help, he conversed with him on what was helpful; but when it came to prayers, he asked him to lead, not being ashamed to learn himself.

Jerome had no vested interest in upholding the supremacy of the hierarchy over the monastic life, yet he too makes a convincing and vivid case for hierarchical structures, if only in the common-sense need for some law and order:

> ep.125.15[17] No art is ever learned without a master. Even dumb animals and wild herds follow leaders of their own. Bees have queens; cranes fly in a Y-formation after one of their number. There is but one emperor; each province has but one judge. Rome was founded by two brothers. But since it could not have two kings simultaneously it resorted at the outset to fratricide... Each church has a single bishop, a single archpresbyter, a single archdeacon, and every ecclesiastical order is subject to its own rulers. A ship has but one pilot, a house but one master, and the largest army moves at the command of one man. That I may not weary you by accumulating instances, my point is: do not follow your own whim; live in a monastery. For there you will be under the control of one father and you will have many companions.

A glimpse of the earliest *modus vivendi* between the monks and the clergy can be seen in *The First Greek Life of Pachomius*:

---

[16]Text: PG 26.957   [17]Text: CSEL 56.133

27 [18] When there was need for the Eucharist, he called in from the nearest churches a priest who made the celebration for them. For among them there was no one invested with the clerical office. He had deliberated on the subject and often told them that it was good not to ask for rank and honor, especially in a community, for fear this should be an occasion for a strife, envy, jealousy, and then schisms to arise in a large community of monks. He told them, 'In the same way as a spark of fire, however small at the beginning, if cast into a threshing-floor and not quickly quenched, destroys the year's labor, so the clerical dignity is the beginning of a temptation to love of power. It is better to be subject modestly to the Church of God and to consider as minister of this sacred rite the one we find at any time and who has been established by our fathers the bishops. In the past also not all the people were Levites. But if a monk from another place is ordained a cleric, we must not—heaven forbid! — vilify him as someone who has been ordained unwillingly. We reckon him an obedient father an an imitator of the saints, if only he performs the service blamelessly.'

The proper relationship with the hierarchical church is stressed in the *Greek Life of Pachomius*[19]:

94 His (Theodore's) orthodoxy is manifest, for he was near the *spring welling up to eternal life* (Jn.4:14), drinking from it so as to bear fruits. We mean the archbishop, not only the archbishop, holy Athanasius, then on the throne, but whoever sat on it. Whoever sits on that throne is not just sitting there alone, but He who said that *where two or three are gathered in his name, he is in their midst* (Mt.18:20), *Christ, the Son of the living God* (Mt.16:16), the Church's foundation and its founder, God and man.

[18]Text: *S. Pachomii Vitae Graecae*, ed. F. Halkin, Subsidia hagiographica., 19, Brussels, 1932; Trans.: A. Veilleux, *Pachomian Koinonia, 1,* Kalamazoo, MI,1980, 314.
[19]Text: Halkin, op.cit.

A little later in the same work, we read an account of an interesting confrontation between Pachomius and the local hierarchy:

> 112 As Pachomius' fame spread far and wide and people talked about him, some would say balanced things, others exaggerated. Once there arose a debate about his being called clairvoyant, and he was summoned to answer the charge in the church of Latopolis in the presence of monks and bishops. He came there with some senior brothers and, seeing those who were contending against him, kept his peace. When he was asked by bishops Philo and Mouei to answer the charge, he replied, 'Were you not once monks with me in the monastery before you became bishops? Do you not know that by the grace of God I, just like you, love Him and care for the brothers.

And he went on to explain that the gift of clairvoyance (which was nothing more than an unerring insight into who were genuine monks and who were mere outward conformists) was, like everything else in his life, a gift of the man-loving God for which he personally deserved no credit.

RENUNCIATION

#46 *At the same time let all realize that while the profession of the evangelical counsels involves the renunciation of goods that undoubtedly deserve to be highly valued, it does not constitute an obstacle to the true development of the human person but by its nature is supremely beneficial to that development.*

Separation from the world, and renunciation of personal possessions, marked the necessary prelude to the search for salvation in primitive monasticism. Renunciation is a key-word in Pachomian literature. "I left you", Pachomius said on his deathbed, "in all humility and in renunciation."[20] 'Renunciation' is also the title of the first of the Discourses of Dorotheus of Gaza, and in it he tells the monks that 'as we are set apart from the world and its affairs, so we ought to be set apart from the desire for material things, and to know what resurrection is, and why we came to the monastery'. He sees the monastic life as a double crucifixion. After offering to God all the other virtues the Fathers offer virginity and poverty as a gift; they crucified the world to themselves, and struggled to crucify themselves to the world.

The superiority of virginity and celibacy to marriage for clerics is eloquently stated in the *Panegyric on St. Basil* by his lifelong friend from student days in Athens, Gregory of Nazianzus:

> 62 [21] A great trait is virginity and celibacy, and to be ranked with the angels, and with non-composite nature — I shrink from saying with Christ's, Who, having willed to be born for us who are born, was born of a virgin, giving the force of law to virginity, to detach us from this life and cut us off from the world, or rather, to put away one world for another, the present for the future.

Gregory pays tribute to Basil for his role in organizing monastic life and rule with special emphasis on virginity:

> Whose are the convents and the written rules by which he subjected all the senses, and regulated all the members, and urged the practice of true virginity, turning the eye of beauty inward from the visible to the invisible, withering away the external and withdrawing the fuel from the flame, but showing what is hidden to God, Who alone is the true bridegroom of souls, Who takes in with Him vigilant souls, if they meet Him with their lamps burning and an abundant supply of oil (cf. Mt. 25:1-13).

[20] See *Dorotheos of Gaza Discourses and Sayings*, Cistercian Studies,33, Kalamazoo, Michigan, 1977

[21] Text: PG 36. 576-577

In Basil's own *Moralia*, Monastic Rule, no. 77[22], we read:

> That virgins should be free from all solicitude for this world so that they may be able to give thanks to God without distraction of mind and body, in expectation of the Kingdom of Heaven.

This rule is based on two Scriptural texts: Mt. 19:12, on the three types of eunuchs, culminating in *some have freely renounced sex for the sake of God's reign* and 1 Cor. 7:32-35: *The unmarried man is busy with the Lord's affairs. . . the virgin — indeed, any unmarried woman — is concerned with things of the Lord, in pursuit of holiness in body and spirit.*

Much of the Fathers' writing about nuns tends to be neurotic and cloistral. The veiling of virgins was a matter of inordinate interest to the Fathers, especially to the Africans, Tertullian and Cyprian. Tertullian devoted a violent polemical treatise to the subject, *On the Veiling of Virgins*. Even in his earlier treatise, *On Prayer*, the subject occupies considerable space:

> 21[23] A point which must be treated, since in general throughout the church it is regarded as an open question, is the question whether or not virgins should be veiled. Those who allow virgins to go uncovered derive support for their view from the fact that the Apostle designated specifically, not that virgins, but that women, are to be veiled (cf. 1 Cor. 11:5: 'But every woman praying or prophesying with her head uncovered disgraces her head'); that is, he referred not to the sex, designating them 'females', but to one group within the sex, naming them 'women.' ...as in the reference to the male sex, under the term 'man' he forbids that even unmarried men should have their heads covered, similarly in reference to the female sex, under the term 'woman' he commands that even a virgin should have her head covered...

[22]Text: PG 31.857   [23]Text: CCL 1.268

'But suppose that someone has consecrated herself to God'. Nevertheless, from this time on, she rearranges her hair and changes her whole appearance to that of a woman. Therefore, let her be earnest about the whole business and present the complete appearance of a virgin; what she conceals for God's sake, let her keep completely out of sight.

When Cyprian came to write his *On the Dress of Virgins*, probably soon after he became bishop of Carthage in 249 A.D., he relied heavily on Tertullian's *On Women's Dress* but he is considerably more urbane and fatherly in his admonitions. He addresses the virgins as 'the flower of ecclesiastical seed, the grace and ornament of spiritual endowment, a joyous disposition, the wholesome, uncorrupted work of praise and honor, God's image answering to the holiness of the Lord, the more illustrious portion of Christ's flock, the glorious fruitfulness of Mother Church.' But he is just as relentless as Tertullian in forbidding cosmetics and jewelry as the invention of the devil, in banning attendance at noisy wedding banquets or promiscuous public bathing places, and in insisting that their dress be plain and unadorned.

12[24] Showy adornments and clothing and the allurements of beauty are not becoming in any except prostitutes and shameless women, and of none, almost, is the dress more costly than of those whose modesty is cheap...

19 You transform the bath into a public show; the place where you are more shameful than the theater. There, all reserve is cast off; the honor and modesty of the body are laid aside together with the clothing; virginity is unveiled to be marked out and contaminated. Now then, consider whether, when she is clothed, such a one is modest among men who has grown in immodesty by the boldness of her nakedness.

21 Listen, therefore, virgins, as to a father; listen, I pray

[24]Text: PSt 34, Washington, DC, 1932, tr. A.E. Keenan

you, to one who fears for you and at the same time warns
you; listen to one who is faithfully watching over your
benefits and interests. Be such as God, the Creator, has
made you; be such as the hand of the Father has fashioned you. Let your countenance remain uncorrupted,
your neck pure, your beauty genuine; let your ears remain
unpierced, your arms and neck unburdened with a costly
chain of bracelets and necklaces; let your feet be free from
fetters of gold, your hair free of tinting or dye; let your
eyes be worthy to see God. Let the baths be frequented
with women who are pure in their lustrations. Let inde-
cent weddings and their wanton banquets be avoided,
contact with which is dangerous. Control your dress, you
who are a virgin; control gold, you who control the flesh
and the world.

St. Augustine gets equally exercised about monks who feel
that they are exempt from the general stricture of St. Paul:
Does not nature itself teach you that for a man to wear his
hair long is degrading? (1 Cor. 11:14). In *The Work of
Monks*:

> 32[25] How lamentably ridiculous it is to bring forward that
> other argument, if argument it is, which they resort to in
> defence of their long hair. They say that the Apostle
> forbade men to wear their hair long, but, they argue,
> those who have castrated themselves for the sake of the
> kingdom of heaven (cf. Mt. 19:12) are no longer men. O
> astonishing madness!... (Here he examines various bibli-
> cal texts with reference to men and women).
> 33 Wherefore, let those who do not wish to act rightly at
> least cease from teaching perversely. There are some who
> by this one fault of wearing their hair long offend and
> disturb the Church, because some of the faithful, not
> wishing to think evil of them, are forced to twist the
> Apostle's words into a perverted interpretation....
> Therefore, we do not chastise them, but we ask and beg,

[25]Text: CSEL 41.591

through the divinity and humanity of Christ and through the charity of the Holy Spirit that they cease to place this stumbling block in the path of the weak for whom Christ died...

Leander of Seville, in his work *The Training of Nuns*, which dates back to the second half of the sixth century, has very explicit directives on the appropriate dress for nuns:

10[26] ...compose your mind inwardly, dearest Florentina, in all ways and adorn it with the flowers of the various virtues. Wear that habit of the mind which will delight the only Son of the heavenly Father, and, neglecting the beauty of the flesh, beautify the mind alone with holy ways; that wherein the carnal please the carnal, you may be all the more displeasing to the eyes of the carnal and you may pursue with all care and diligence the contemplation of the divine that renders you beautiful. For then you will be truly adorned if you love, not the outer, but the inner habit; and then you will be well dressed if you have tried to attain resplendence of mind rather than flashiness of garments.

Do not wear stunning clothes, anything having a pleat; for the eye is curious before and behind, and do not wear dresses that billow. Be careful of clothes carefully and diligently patterned and bought at a very high price, for that is care of the flesh, that is the eager desire of the eyes. Rather wear the sort of clothing that will not attract the attention of men to you or make you noticeable to them, but which will prove you innocent before God; that the integrity of a good mind may be recognized through the simplicity of your habit.

PERSEVERANCE IN EXCELLENCE

#47 *Let everyone called to the profession of the counsels take earnest care to persevere and excel still more in the life to which God has called them.*

[26]Text: *Analecta Bollandiana* 67 (1949) 407-424; cf. FOTC 62.204

St. Augustine, in The Work of Monks, takes up the question of monks who want to be exempt from manual labor in order to concentrate on prayer, chanting the psalms, reading, and the word of God. He shows how all these various activities can be co-ordinated in a full and satisfying life:

> XVII. 20[27] ... if the exigencies of our physical weakness make it imperative for the servants of God to be free to attend to these duties at certain times, why do we not allot other periods for the fulfillment of the apostolic precepts? One prayer of an obedient man is heard more quickly than ten thousand prayers of a disobedient one. In fact, persons who are engaged in manual labor can easily sing divine canticles and lighten the labor itself, with God, so to speak, calling the beat for His oarsmen. Are we unaware of the vanities and frequently even the baseness to which theatrical producers devote their hearts and their tongues, even though their hands do not cease from work?
>
> What, therefore, hinders the servant of God from meditating on the law of God and from singing to the name of the Lord most high while he performs manual labor, provided that he have time set aside for learning the psalms he is later to sing from memory?

[27]Text: CSEL 41.564

VII

The Eschatological Nature of the Pilgrim Church and Her Union with the Heavenly Church

#48 *The Church...will receive its perfection only in the glory of heaven, when will come the time of the renewal of all things (cf. Acts 3:21).*

The opening sentence in Peter Brown, *The Cult of the Saints* (Chicago 1981) is an apt description of the seventh chapter of *Lumen Gentium*: "This is about the joining of Heaven and earth, and the role, in this joining, of dead human beings." What faith calls upon Christians to believe and to act upon is the possibility of a beneficial communication between the members of the pilgrim church on earth and the blessed in Heaven, between the church militant and the church triumphant, the two parts of the church which will ultimately become one in the final restoration of all things in Christ.

The notion of *peregrinatio*, pilgrimage, is already found in St. Paul: "knowing that while we are in the body we are exiles (*peregrinamur*) from the Lord" (2 Cor. 5:6). The Epistle to the Hebrews also reminds us that on earth we have no permanent home, but we are seekers after the city which is to come (Heb. 13:14). The resulting restlessness, part of the paradox and the tension of being a Christian, is splendidly caught in *The Epistle to Diognetus*:

5.2[1] They live, each in his native land, but as though they were not really at home there. They share in all duties like citizens and suffer all hardships like strangers. Each foreign land is for them a native land, and every native land a foreign land.... They dwell on earth, but they are citizens of heaven.

Clement of Alexandria warned in the *Paidagogos* (3.41,1, SC 158.90) that we have no fatherland on earth so that we may learn to despise earthly possessions, and in the *Protreptikos* (10.108, SC 2.176) he says: 'If you enrol yourself as one of God's people, Heaven is your country, God your legislation'. Augustine says that the Church 'like a pilgrim in a foreign land presses forward amid the persecutions of the world and the consolations of God' (*City of God* XVIII.51.2).

It is noteworthy how frequently Augustine returns to the notion of a pilgrim church, despite his insistence on the spread of the church world-wide. The Church here below remains provisional, nostalgic, precarious and impermanent.

32.9[2] We are born and die here; let us not love this; let us migrate by charity, by that charity by which we love God. In this pilgrimage of our life we meditate on the fact that we shall not always be here but by living the good life we shall prepare for ourselves a place there from which we shall never migrate. (*Tract. on John*)

85.24[3] This is the land of the dead. The land of the dead will pass, the land of the living will come. In the land of the dead here there is toil, grief, fear, tribulation, temptation, groaning, sighing; here the happy ones are false, the unhappy, true, because happiness is false, unhappiness true... Blessed are they that mourn. Wherefore blessed? In hope. Wherefore mourning? In act. For they mourn in this death, in these tribulations, in their pilgrim state,

---

[1]Text: SC 33.62   [2]Text: CCL 36.305   [3]Text: CCL 39.1196

because they recognize their state of misery and mourning they are blessed. (*Enarr. in Ps.*)

Theodore of Mopsuestia sees baptismal initiation to church membership as a prefigure of our ultimate enrollment in Heaven:

> 11 [4] He who now desires to approach the gift of baptism is presented to the church of God which our Lord, the Anointed One, shows to the faithful as a certain prefigure of these heavenly things in this world when he says to Peter, 'Thou art Peter, and upon this rock I will build my church!.. (Mt. 16:18-19). The Anointed One shows that He has given as a prefigure of heavenly things the Church itself which has the capacity of making one familiar with the church familiar also with heavenly things, and a stranger to it likewise estranged from the things of heaven.
>
> Next, it is assuredly to those at the head of the Church that the government of the Church has been confided, and it is those to whom the word addressed to the blessed Peter who have the keys of the kingdom of Heaven, and what they bind on earth is bound also in Heaven, and what they loose on earth is loosed also in Heaven. Not that men are responsible for this, but because the Church has received this power from God.

And again later:

> 17 In this world here by the regeneration of baptism in the Church which is called the body of Christ we receive in a figure association with Him; but in the world to come this figure will be fully realized since 'this humble body of ours will be transformed to resemble His glorious body' (Phil. 3:21).

Caesarius of Arles has an extended reflection on the two

[4]Text: *Studi e Testi*, 145; cf. A Mingana, Woodbrooke Studies, vol. VI, Cambridge, 1933, 23, 69.

cities, similarly wistful, almost mystically penetrating, in its far-reaching concept of church in time and eternity:

> s.151[5] Nothing prevents you and us from always being united in love and charity even though we only see each other in the flesh occasionally. For in this world's sojourn we could not be always together, even if we could be in the same city, for the city where good Christians will never be separated from one another is a very different kind of city.
>
> There are two cities, dearest brethren. The first is the city of this world, the second, the city of paradise. The good Christian is always journeying in the city of the world, but he is recognized as a citizen of the city of paradise. The first city is full of labor, the second, is restful; the first is full of misery, the second, blessed; in the first there is labor, in the second repose; if a man lives sinfully in the first he cannot arrive in the second. We must be pilgrims in this world in order to merit to be citizens of heaven. If one wants to love this world and remain a citizen of it, he has no place in heaven, for we prove our pilgrim status by our longing for our true country. Let no one deceive himself, beloved brethren; the true country of Christians is in heaven, not here. The city of Christians, their blessed state, their true, eternal happiness is not here. The one who searches for happiness in this world will not find it in heaven. Our true fatherland is paradise, our city of Jerusalem is the heavenly one. The angels are our fellow-citizens; our parents are the patriarchs and prophets; the apostles and martyrs, our king is Christ. May we live, therefore, in this earthly sojourn in a manner that will enable us to long for such a country during our stay here, for if a man wants to lead a sinful life he will be incapable of longing for that country. Now there has gone before us to that country the multitude of patriarchs and prophets, and the glorious army of apostles and martyrs, myriads of confessors and virgins,

---

[5]Text: CCL 104.617

and a host of the faithful. All of these already established in blessed rest daily await us with the outstretched arms of their love. In their longings and their prayers it is equally their wish to receive us with triumph and exultation into that land of paradise when we have overcome the world in our fight against the devil.

St. Augustine, in *The City of God*, says:

> XVIII.51[6] In evil days like these, the Church walks onward like a wayfarer stricken by the world's hostility, but comforted by the mercy of God. Nor does this state of affairs date only from the days of Christ's and His apostles' presence on earth. It was never any different from the days when the first just man, Abel, was slain by his ungodly brother. So it shall continue until this world no longer exists.

In *Homily 16, on Psalm 83*[7], Jerome has personal eschatological reflections on 'How lovely are your tabernacles, O Lord of hosts...the sparrow finds himself a home':

> 'How lovely are your tabernacles, O Lord of hosts!' Some people's sole ambition is to possess property; others long to be enriched with the world's wealth; still others wish to attain prominent positions in assemblies and be esteemed among men. But for me, there is only one longing: to see Your eternal dwellings. To me, these are the lovely dwellings — where the virtuous, not the wicked, congregate. 'My soul yearns and pines for the courts of the Lord.' This is my one desire, my one love, that I may see Your courts. Note the order. First, the Psalmist longs for the tabernacles, tents without a foundation, and easily portable. A tent, moreover, is always mobile, folded up, and carried hither and thither. Courts, on the other hand, although certainly not houses, do have a sort of foundation, and from the court we enter the house. The Psalmist, there-

---

[6] Text: CSEL 40.2353   [7] Text: CCL 78.97

fore, at first longs for the tabernacle; then he pines and
yearns for the sight of your courts, and, when he is in your
court, he finally exclaims, 'Happy are they who dwell in
your house.'

'Even the sparrow finds himself a house, and the turtle-
dove a nest.' ... The birds that fly to and fro without
restraint, after their flight, have a place and a nest in
which to rest. How much more ought not my body and
soul procure for itself a resting place?

The turtle-dove is a chaste bird. It never makes its
abode in lowly places, but always builds its nest high up in
lofty tree tops. As the birds of purity, the sparrow and the
turtle make their nests in the higher places, so the tabernacles, courts and houses are not in this lowly earth, but
on high in the kingdom of Heaven.

COMMUNION BETWEEN HEAVEN AND EARTH

#49 ... *the union of the wayfarers with the brethren who
sleep in the peace of Christ is in no way interrupted, but on
the contrary, ... this union is reinforced by an exchange of
spiritual goods.*

In Origen, *On Prayer* we read:

> 11.2[8] Now the one great virtue according to the Word of
> God is love of one's neighbor. We must believe that the
> saints who have died possess this love in a far higher
> degree towards the ones engaged in the combat of life
> than those who are still subject to human weakness and
> involved in the combat along with their weaker brethren.
> The words "If one member suffer anything, all the
> members suffer with it, or if one member glory, all the
> members rejoice with it" (1 Cor. 12:26) are not confined
> to those on earth who love their brethren. For the words
> apply just as much to the love of those who have left this
> present life ... "the solicitude for all the churches. Who is

[8] Text: GCS Origenes 2.322; cf. ACW 19.44, tr.J.J.O'Meara

weak, and I am not weak? Who is scandalized and I am
not inflamed?" (2 Cor. 11:28-29).

And Christ Himself agrees with this, saying that He is
sick with each of the saints who are sick, likewise with
those in prison and naked, and a stranger, and hungry
and thirsty... (cf.Mt.25:35-40). If the angels of God came
to Jesus and ministered to Him (Mt. 4:11), and if we
should not believe that this ministry of the angels to Jesus
was limited to a short time during His earthly sojourn
...how many angels do you think minister to Jesus to
gather together the sons of Israel one by one, and assemble those of the dispersion, and saves them that are in fear
and call upon Him? And do they not contribute more
than the Apostles to the growth and increase of the
Church, so that John says in the Apocalypse that certain
angels preside over the churches?

St. Augustine, in his *Eight Questions of Dulcitius*, utilises
an answer already given by him in *Faith, Hope and Charity*,
on the question whether an offering made for the dead is of
any profit for their souls:

> Q.2⁹ 'The time, moreover,' I say, 'which intervenes
> between the death of a man and the final resurrection
> detains souls in hidden abodes as each deserves either of
> peace or tribulation according as it has chosen while it
> lived in the flesh. No one should deny that the souls of the
> dead are relieved by the piety of their living relatives,
> when the sacrifice of their Mediator is offered for them,
> or when alms are given in the Church. But these things are
> profitable to those who, when alive, merited that they
> could be profitable afterwards. For there is a way of
> living that is neither so good that it does not need those
> things after death nor so evil that these things are not
> profitable after death. Therefore all merit is prepared
> here by which anyone can be relieved or burdened in the
> afterlife.'

⁹Text: PL40.158

Augustine puts the same thought in more purely autobiographical terms in the *Confessions*:

> IX.37[10] Therefore, let her rest in peace with her husband: he was her first and only marriage partner, and she obeyed him with endurance bringing fruit to thee so that she might win him for thee. And inspire, my Lord, my God, inspire thy servants, my brothers, thy sons, my lords, who with voice and heart and writings I serve, that as many of them as shall read these Confessions may also at thy altar remember Monica, thy handmaid, together with Patricius, her husband.

The intercessory aspect of the communion of saints can be seen at work in the Christian community of Lyons in France in the last quarter of the second century. The *Letter to the Churches of Vienne and Lyons* (the text of which is preserved in Eusebius, *Church History*, Book V) describes a brutal anti-Christian uprising in Gaul in 177 A.D. The vibrant faith of this largely immigrant church (they were settlers from Asia Minor and Phrygia and are writing back in Greek to their brethren in the Middle East) is obviously linked with advocacy of the Holy Spirit and the extension of the advocacy role to individual Christians. One of their martyrs is described as follows[11]:

> Called the Christian's advocate, he possessed the Advocate within him, the Spirit that filled Zachary, which he demonstrated by the fullness of his love, consenting as he did to lay down his life.

The sense of the strength and interaction of community prayer is corroborated by certain statements in the contemporary writings of Irenaeus of Lyons, who stresses the concept of advocate, and the advocacy role of the Virgin Mary, in the following excerpt from his *Demonstration*:

[10]Text: CCL 27.154   [11]Text: OECT, tr. H. Musurillo, 64

33 [12] And just as it was through a virgin who disobeyed
that man was stricken, fell and died, so, too, it was
through the Virgin who obeyed the Word of God that
man, resuscitated by life, received life. For the Lord came
to seek the sheep that was lost, and it was man who was
lost. Therefore He did not become some other formation,
but He likewise, of her that was descended from Adam,
preserved a similar human formation; for Adam of necessity had to be restored in Christ, that mortality might be
swallowed up in immortality, and Eve in Mary, so that a
Virgin, become the advocate of a virgin, might undo and
destroy the disobedience of a virgin by a Virgin's
obedience.

THE CULT OF THE SAINTS

#50 *The Church has always believed that the apostles and
Christ's martyrs. . .are closely united with us in Christ; she
has always venerated them, together with the Blessed Virgin
Mary and the holy angels, with a special love. . .*

The cult of the saints does not detract in any way from
worship due to God alone. St. Augustine says: 'We do not
stop praising God when we praise His works and marvel at
the struggles in which He engaged in the persons of His
dedicated soldiers (On the Birthday of the Martyr Cyprian,
313). Augustine also points out that the martyrs because of
their union with Christ became in turn true intercessors
without in any way minimising the intercessory role of
Christ:

> [13] The martyrs have departed from this world with such a
> high degree of perfection that instead of being in need of
> our assistance, they are in a position to help us. Their role
> as our advocates however is not based on their own
> personal power but on that person to whom they adhere
> as perfect members.

[12]Trans. cf. ACW 16.69, ed. Smith   [13]Text: PL 38.1423

Canonized saints are venerated both on account of their union and conformity with Christ, and for their ecclesial importance as continuing members of the Body of Christ. As St. Augustine puts it:

> [14]When we speak to God in prayer for mercy, we do not separate the Son from Him, and when the Body of the Son prays, it does not separate its Head from itself; and it is one Savior of His Body, our Lord, Jesus Christ, the Son of God, who both prays for us, and prays in us, and is prayed to by us. (*Enarr. in Ps.*,85).

More particularly, in his *Care for the Dead*, Augustine devotes an entire treatise to the cult of the dead, based on the assumption that 'it is the practice of the universal church to pray for their dead, stemming from the sacrifice offered for the dead in Maccabees (2 Macc.12:43), and 'the authority of the universal church which clearly favors the practice'.

St. Jerome, in his *Against Vigilantius* is obviously involved in a very live debate about the value, if any, of the intercession of the saints:

> 6 [15] You say in your tract that as long as we are alive we can pray for one another, but once we are dead nobody's prayers for another can be heard, and all the more so because the martyrs, though they cry out for their blood to be avenged, have never been able to have their request granted. If apostles and martyrs, while still alive, can pray for others while they should still be concerned about themselves, how much more should they do so when they have won their crowns, overcome and triumphed?
>
> A single man, Moses, often wins pardon from God for six hundred thousand armed men (cf. Exod. 32). Stephen, the follower of the Lord and the first Christian martyr, entreats pardon for his persecutors; and, when

---

[14]Text: CCL 39.1176

[15]Text: PL 23.344; cf. ANF ser.2, VI.419

once they have entered on their life with Christ, shall they have less power than before? The apostle, Paul, says that souls were given to him in the ship; after his demise, when he has begun to be with Christ, must he keep his mouth shut and be unable to utter a word for those who have believed his gospel throughout the whole world?

Shall Vigilantius, the live dog, be better than Paul, the dead lion? I should be right in saying so with Ecclesiastes if I admitted that Paul is dead in spirit. But the truth is that the saints are not regarded as dead, but are said to be asleep.

Lumen Gentium reminds us that from the very earliest days the Church has honored with great respect the memory of the dead and instances the inscriptions from the Catacombs as evidence. Here are a few of them, selected at random[16]:

Eucharis is my mother and Pius my father. Brethren, when you assemble here together to implore and pray to the Father and to the Son, I entreat you to make remembrance of dear Agape that Almighty God may take her forever to His glory. (Cemetery of Priscilla)

O Atticus, sleep in peace and in the security of thy salvation and pray earnestly for our sins (Capitol Museum)

Gentianus, faithful, in peace who lived twelve years, eight months and sixteen days. You will intercede for us in your prayers because we know that you are in Christ. (Lateran Museum)

PASTORAL CONCLUSIONS

#51 *Let us teach the faithful that the authentic cult of the saints does not consist so much in a multiplicity of external acts, but rather in a more intense practice of our love,*

---

[16]O. Marucchi, *The Evidence of the Catacombs*, New York, 1929,48,56,57

whereby . . . we seek from the saints 'example in their way of life, fellowship in their communion, and the help of their intercession' (Mass Preface).

It is necessary to stress the concept of authenticity in regard to the cult of the saints because of the many abuses that were associated with it from earliest times. Assemblies and banquets at tombs, pilgrimages and the circulation of relics led to many abuses. Already in Augustine's *On the Work of Monks* mendicant wanderers are criticised for trafficking in martyrs' relics, if indeed they were always martyrs.

The cult of martyrs indeed predated the cult of saints in the early church and here we quote a piece of very early evidence, from the *Martyrdom of Polycarp*, which indicates the decent dimensions of such a cult:

> 18.2[17] We have at last gathered his bones. . . and laid them to rest. . . . And if it is possible for us to assemble again, may God grant us to celebrate the anniversary of his martyrdom with gladness, thus to recall the memory of those who fought in the glorious combat, and to teach and strengthen by his example those who shall come after us.

Gregory of Nyssa, in his work, *On Pilgrimages*[17], stresses that change of place is less important in spiritual progress than change of heart.

> ep.2 Change of place does not affect any closer attachment to God. Irrespective of where you are, God will come to you if the rooms of your soul are found suitable for His occupation. But if you keep your interior full of wicked thoughts, even if you were on Golgotha, or on the Mount of Olives, even if you stood on the memorial-rock of the Resurrection, you will be as removed from receiving Christ into your interior as one who has not even started to confess Him.

[17]Text: OECT, ed., Musurillo, *The Acts of the Christian Martyrs*, 16.

Gregory of Nyssa, although he himself had visited the Holy Land, more than once stresses the priority of interior dispositions over external acts. In a letter to three women in Jerusalem after he had returned to Cappadocia from a visit there, he stresses that their holy way of life was as inspirational for him as his actual visit to the holy places:

> ep. 3[18] Meeting with good and beloved friends and visiting the memorials of the Lord's enormous love for us mortals in your locality has been a source of intense joy and gladness to me. The lustre of these holidays has been two-fold, first, viewing the salutary symbols of the God who conferred life on us, and secondly meeting with souls in whom the tokens of the Lord's grace are to be discerned with such clarity that one can believe that Bethlehem, Golgotha and Olivet and the scene of the Resurrection are really in the heart that embraces God.
>
> For when Christ has been formed in one through a good conscience, when one has nailed down the promptings of the flesh and has become crucified to Christ by reverential fear, when one has rolled back from oneself the heavy stone of earthly illusions, when one has emerged from the grave of the body and begun to walk as it were in newness of life, abandoning this low-lying valley of human life and ascending with a soaring desire to that heavenly country with all its elevated thoughts, the abode of Christ, no longer feeling the burden of the flesh, but elevating it by chastity so that the flesh, with nebulous weightlessness accompanies the ascending soul — such a one, I feel, is to be numbered among those illustrious ones in whom the memorials of the Lord's love for humanity is to be seen.
>
> When, then, I saw with my own eyes not just the Holy Places themselves but also saw the tokens of places like them manifest in yourselves as well I was filled with indescribable joy.

[18] Text: PG 46.1016

VIII

Our Lady and the Church

I. Introduction

#52 Joined to Christ the head and in communion with all his saints, the faithful must in the first place reverence the memory of "the glorious ever Virgin Mary, Mother of God and of our Lord, Jesus Christ."

Hugo Rahner has well observed: 'We need to learn once more what was so treasured by the early Church: to learn to see the Church in our Lady and our Lady in the Church'. This special relationship developed against the theological backdrop of the all-sufficiency of Christ as the one mediator; 'for there is but one God and one mediator of God and men, the man, Christ Jesus, who gave himself a redemption for many' (1 Tim. 2:5-6). As Origen described this central, all-sufficient role of Christ in ecclesial dynamics:

> 6.48[1] Just as the soul moves the body which has not been endowed to be moved in a vital manner by itself, so the Word energizing the whole body keeps the Church in motion and each of its several parts.

Mary's growing cult in early Christianity was often viewed wrongly as posing a threat to Christ's sole mediatorship.

[1] Text: *Contra Celsum* (SC 147.300)

Mary's title of 'Mother of God' came under attack from Nestorius who was Patriarch of Constantinople in 428. Objecting to Mary being venerated as *Theotokos* (Mother of God) he proposed that 'if anyone says that Mary is the Mother of God the Logos, and not rather the mother of Him who is Emmanuel, let him be anathema'. In Greek terminology he wanted her to be called *Christotokos* (Christ-bearer), but not *Theotokos* (God-bearer). He had argued himself into this position from his attempt to explain the union of the two natures, human and divine, in Christ. His explanation was that God the Logos and Jesus Christ were two distinct persons united morally but not physically in the person called Christ.

The Christological controversies of the 4th century with their Mariological reverberations eventually found a resolution in the Councils of Constantinople (381), Ephesus (431) and Chalcedon (451). Much of the contemporary confusions about Mary are heard echoing in a Letter of Gregory of Nazianzus:

> 101 [2] If anyone does not accept holy Mary as Mother of God, he is cut off from the deity. If anyone should say that Christ passed through the Virgin as through a conduit, and was not fashioned in a way that is divine as well as human...he is equally godless.
>
> If anyone should say that the man was first fashioned and only afterwards did God steal in, he is also to be condemned. If anyone introduces two Sons, one of God the Father and the other of the Mother, and not one and the same Son, may he forfeit his share in the adoption.

A long excerpt from Vincent of Lerins will help us to see the *Theotokos* debate in its historical context[3]:

> Apollinaris boasts of acquiescing in the doctrine of the Unity of the Trinity — although not in the full purity of the faith. But he blasphemes openly with regard to the

[2]Text: SC 208.42   [3]Text: PL 50.654

Incarnation of the Lord. He says that either there was no human soul in the body of our Saviour, or, if there were one, that it had neither mind nor reason.

He asserts that the flesh of our Lord was not formed from the flesh of Holy Virgin Mary, but descended from Heaven into the Virgin, and he taught, in constant wavering and doubt, sometimes that she was co-eternal with God the Word, sometimes that she was only created out of the divinity of the Word. He refused to admit two substances in Christ — one divine, the other human; one from the Father, the other from the Mother.

He believed that the Word's nature was itself divided, as though the one remained in God and the other had been converted into flesh, whereas the truth says that the one Christ consists of two substances. Apollinaris, contrary to truth, asserts that from one Divinity of Christ two substances were made. So much for Apollinaris.

Nestorius, who suffered from a disease quite contrary to Apollinaris, suddenly introduced two persons while pretending to distinguish two substances in Christ. In his unheard-of wickedness he assumes that there are two sons of God — two christs — the one, God, the other, man; one, begotten of the Father, the other, of the mother. Thus he asserts that Holy Mary is not to be called *Theotokos* but *Christotokos*, since she gave birth not to Christ-God but to Christ-man.

"When the fullness of time came, God sent His Son, born of a woman that we might receive the adoption of sons" (Gal. 4: 4-5).
Stressing both the unique role of Christ and the necessary role of Mary in Redemption, Ignatius of Antioch, writing *to the Ephesians*, says:

> 7.2[4] There is only one Physician, both carnal and spiritual, born and unborn, God become man, true life in death; sprung both from Mary and from God, first sub-

[4]SC 10.64

ject to suffering and then incapable of it —Jesus Christ Our Lord.

In a powerful image Proclus of Constantinople, in a homily[5] delivered before Nestorius, probably in the year 429, described Mary as 'the loom of the Incarnation':

> We have been assembled by the holy Mary, that undefiled treasury of virginity, the spiritual paradise, the second Adam, the workshop of the union of the two natures, the market place for the salvific exchange, the bridal chamber wherein the Word espoused flesh..the most pure fleece of heavenly rain (Judg. 6:37), from which the Shepherd clothed the sheep — handmaid and Mother, Virgin and heaven, the only bridge of God to men.
>
> She is the awe-inspiring loom of our Incarnation, whereon in an ineffable manner was woven the garment of the hypostatic union, with the Holy Spirit as weaver; the overshadowing power from above, the connecting thread; the ancient fleece of Adam, the wool; the undefiled flesh from the Virgin, the threaded woof; the shuttle, the immeasurable grace of her who bore, with the Logos as the Artist.

MOTHER OF GOD, MOTHER OF THE REDEEMER

#53 The Virgin Mary...is acknowledged and honored as being truly the Mother of God and of the Redeemer... Wherefore she is hailed as pre-eminent and as a wholly unique member of the Church, and as its type and outstanding model in faith and charity.

Lumen Gentium is similar in structure to Henri de Lubac's seminal work *The Splendor of the Church*: it begins with the Church as mystery and ends with the Church and Our Lady. Mary's important role in Christ's plan of salva-

[5]ACO I.1.1.103

tion is well expressed by Ignatius of Antioch in his *Epistle to the Ephesians*:

> 18.2[6] For our God, Jesus the Christ, was conceived by Mary, in God's plan being sprung from the seed of David and from the Holy Spirit. He was born and baptized that by His passion He might hallow water. 19. Now Mary's virginity and her giving birth escaped the notice of the prince of this world, as did the Lord's death — those three secrets crying to be told but wrought in God's silence.

Against the Docetists, who held that Christ had only an apparent, but not a real human body, Ignatius found it necessary to emphasize this reality:

> Stop your ears, therefore, when anyone speaks to you that stands apart from Jesus Christ, from David's scion and Mary's Son, who was really born, and ate and drank, was truly persecuted under Pontius Pilate, was truly crucified and died. . . who was also truly raised from the dead (ad Trall. 9.1[7])

Augustine, in *On Holy Virginity*, expresses well Mary's pre-eminent role in the Church:

> 6.6[8] That one woman, therefore, is both Mother and Virgin, not only in spirit but also in body. She is mother, indeed, not of our Head, who is our Saviour Himself, of whom she was rather born spiritually, since all who believe in Him (among whom she too is included) are rightly called children of the bridegroom, but she is evidently the mother of us who are His members, because she has co-operated by charity that the faithful, who are members of that Head, might be born in the Church. Indeed she is Mother of the Head Himself in the body. It was fitting that our Head be born of a virgin according to the flesh, for the sake of a wonderful miracle by which He

[6]Text: SC 10.72   [7]Text: SC 10.100   [8]Text: CSEL 41.239; cf. FOTC 27.149

might signify that His members would be born according to the spirit of a virgin, the Church.

Mary alone, therefore, is mother and virgin both in spirit and in body, both Mother of Christ and Virgin of Christ. The Church, on the other hand, in the saints who are to possess the kingdom of God, is indeed wholly the mother of Christ, wholly the virgin of Christ in spirit; in the body, however, not as a whole, but in some she is a virgin of Christ, in others a mother, but not Christ's mother.

Lumen Gentium just stops short of calling Mary the Mother of the Church. There are plenty of patristic precedents for doing so. Epiphanius, for instance, calls Mary the Virgin Mother of Christ, 'the mother of the living'. And the evidence for the title is implicit in two doctrines of Irenaeus: recapitulation and the Eve/Mary parallel. Augustine is quite explicit in *On the Words of the Gospel of Matthew*: Mary is a part of the Church, a holy member, an excellent member, a super-eminent member, but nonetheless a member. . . .

THE BLESSED VIRGIN AND THE MYSTICAL BODY

#54 . . . *the role of the Blessed Virgin in the mystery of the Incarnate Word and the Mystical Body, and the duties of the redeemed towards the Mother of God, who is mother of Christ and mother of men. . . who occupies a place in the Church which is the highest after Christ and also closest to us.*

Recently published fragments of Melito of Sardis[9] illustrate second century belief in Mary's role in our Redemption:

XIII. For this reason the Father sent His incorporeal Son from heaven so that, enfleshed in the Virgin's womb and

---

[9] Text: OECT, ed. Stuart Hall, 80,81,87,xxiv-xxix

born as man, He might bring man to life and gather his parts which death had scattered when he divided man.

XIV. For this cause He came to us; for this cause, though incorporeal, He wove Himself a body of our texture. He was seen as a lamb, but remained a shepherd, carried in the womb by Mary and clothed with His Father; treading the earth and filling Heaven.

New Frag. 11:4: He put on a body from a virgin because of man;
he who is Word with you;
and God is Word,
and Word is Man, and Man is God.
For God visited his own creation, which He had made in his image and likeness. He sent out his own Son from heaven to earth incorporeal, and he took a body from a virgin. He was born a man and he raised up lost man and gathered his scattered members.

And why does Christ die? Was there no need for the judgement of death?... Or why did he become man? Was he not God? Or why did he descend to earth? Was he not King in heaven? Why did it concern God, descent to earth, and conception in the body from the virgin, and wrapping in swathes, and laying in a manger, and sucking milk in a mother's bosom, and baptism in Jordan by John, and mockery on the wood of the cross, and burial in earth, and resurrection from the dead on the third day, and the building of the churches? What was the concern for man? But so that those lost men might be saved, thou hast given thyself for redemption, soul for soul, and body for body, and blood for blood, man for man, and death for death.

Leo the Great, in his *Epistle to Flavian*, draws out the theological implications of the credal formulae: We believe in one God the Father almighty, and in Jesus Christ, His only Son, our Lord, who was born of the Holy Spirit and the Virgin Mary:

ep. 28[10] By these three statements the stratagems of almost all heretics are overthrown. For not only is God believed to be both Almighty and the Father, but the Son is shown to be co-eternal with Him, differing in nothing from Him because He is *God from God*, Almighty from Almighty, and being born from the Eternal One is co-eternal with Him, not posterior in point of time, not dissimilar in glory, not divided in essence, but at the same time the Only Begotten of the Eternal Father was born eternal of the Holy Spirit and the Virgin Mary.

And this nativity, which occurred in time, took nothing away from, and added nothing to, that divine, eternal birth, but expended itself wholly on the restoration of man who had been deceived, in order that he might both vanquish death and overthrow by his strength the devil who possessed the power of death. For we should be now incapable of overcoming the author of sin and death unless He took our nature upon Himself and made it His own whom neither sin could contaminate nor death confine. Without doubt, then, He was conceived of the Holy Spirit within the womb of His Virgin Mother who brought Him forth without the loss of her virginity just as she conceived Him while preserving that virginity.

Ephraim of Syria triumphantly hymns the glories of Mary, truly Mother of God:

Hymn 18[11] Awake, O my harp, your strings, in praise of Mary the Virgin. Lift up your voice and sing the generation, utterly marvellous, of this Virgin, David's daughter, who has brought forth life to the world.

The lover with admiration marvels at her, while the curious enquirer is covered with shame and his ear is stopped up lest he should dare to pry into the Mother who brought forth in virginity inviolate...

[10]Text: PL 54.758

[11]Translation, with modifications, P.Palmer, *Mary in the Documents of the Church*, 16.

In Mary's womb He who from eternity is equal to the Father became an infant. He gave us a share in His own greatness and He Himself took a share in our weakness. He was made mortal along with us so that, by infusing His life into us, we might die no more...

Mary is the garden upon which the rain of blessings descended from the Father. From that rain she herself sprinkled the face of Adam. Thereupon he returned to life and arose from the sepulchre — he who had been buried in hell by his enemies...

Lo, a virgin is become a mother, preserving virginity with its seals broken... She is made God's mother and is at the same time a servant, and the work of his wisdom.

The Virgin who gave birth to the only-begotten has nurtured God and Man, has become Mother of the hidden little one, who was born perfect of the Father and is made an infant in her womb.

St. Augustine, in his sermon 291,[12] On the Birthday of John the Baptiser, gives an extended commentary on Mary's title: 'full of grace':

What art thou, Mary, thou who will presently bring forth? Whence hast thou merited, whence obtained this favor? Whence is it that He who made thee will be made in thee? Whence, I ask, does this great gift come to thee? Thou art a virgin, thou art holy, thou art bound by a vow.

True, thou has merited much, or rather, thou hast received much. But how hast thou merited it? He who made thee is being made within thee. He is made within thee by Him who made thee thyself, or rather should I say by whom heaven and earth were made, by whom all things were made. The Word of God is made flesh within thee by taking flesh, not by losing divinity. The Word is joined to flesh. The Word is wedded to flesh, and the bridal chamber of this exalted marriage is thy womb.

[12]Text: PL 38.1319

Let me repeat, the bridal chamber of this exalted marriage between the Word and flesh is thy womb, whence 'he, the bridegroom goes forth from his bridal chamber' (Ps. 18:6). He finds thee a virgin at his conception. He leaves thee a virgin at His birth. He gives thee fecundity. He does not take away thy integrity. Whence is this to thee?...

"Dost thou ask of me whence is this? I blush to answer thy questions as to my blessedness. Rather listen to the angel's situation. . . . Let the angel reply." Tell me, Angel, whence has Mary this? I already replied when I saluted her: 'Hail, full of grace' (Lk. 1:28)

II. The Role of the Blessed Virgin in the Plan of Salvation

#55 *The sacred writings of the Old and New Testaments, as well as venerable tradition, show the role of the Mother of the Saviour in the plan of salvation in an ever clearer light.*

Even the Old Testament has presentiments of Mary's role in the history of salvation. Ambrose, in his *Jacob and the Happy Life*, writes:

11,7.32[13]But Jacob esteemed compassion with a forbearance that was moral, or he foresaw, with an understanding that was mystical, the mystery of the Church that would be gathered together from the nations. Therefore God's answer was given to Jacob, who prophesied the coming of the Lord Jesus: 'Arise and go to Bethel' (Gen. 35:1), that is, to the house of bread, where Christ was born, as the prophet Michea gives testimony when he says, 'And you, Bethlehem, house of Ephrata, are not too little to be among the first of Juda. For out of you will come forth the ruler in Israel, and his going forth is from the beginning, from the days of eternity' (Mich. 5:1). Truly that is the house of bread, which is the house of

---

[13]Text: CSEL 32.50; cf. FOTC 65.165, tr.M.P.McHugh

Christ, who came to us from Heaven as the bread of salvation so that now no one may be hungry but each one may gain for himself the food of immortality.

And for Ambrose always (cf. *Luc.* 2:7, PL 15.1555) Mary is well bethrothed but a virgin, because she is a type of the Church.

Likewise she is the virgin who shall conceive and bear a son, whose name will be called Emmanuel (cf.Isa.7:14...).

Tertullian discusses this text at some length in his work, *On the Flesh of Christ.*

> 17.2[14] Now it will first be necessary to show what previous reason there was for the Son of God's being born of a virgin. He who was going to consecrate a new order of generation must Himself be born after a novel fashion, concerning which Isaiah foretold how the Lord Himself would give the sign. What, then, is the sign? *Behold a virgin shall conceive and bear a son (cf. Isa 7:14)*. Accordingly, a virgin did conceive and bear "*Emmanuel, God with us*". This is the new generation: a man is born in God.
>
> And in this man God was born, taking the flesh of an ancient race, without the help, however, of the ancient seed, in order that He might reform it with a new seed, that is, in a spiritual fashion, and cleanse it by the removal of all its ancient stains. But the whole of this new generation was prefigured, as in all other instances, in ancient typology, the Lord being born as man by a dispensation in which a virgin was the medium. The earth was still in a virgin state, untilled as yet by any human labor, with no seed as yet cast into its furrows, when, as we are told, God made man from it into a living soul.
>
> As, then, the first Adam is introduced to us, it is reasonable to conclude that the second Adam, likewise, as the

[14]Text: CCL 2.904

apostle has told us, was formed by God into a living spirit out of the ground, in other words, out of a flesh which was sustained as yet by no human generation.

St. Peter Chrysologus deftly expresses the role of Mary's maternity in the plan of salvation in one of his homilies:

> 146.7[15] Mary is called mother. And when is Mary not a mother? 'The gathering together of the waters he called seas (*maria*) ' (Gen. 1:10). Was it not she who conceived in her single womb the people going out from Egypt, that it might come forth a heavenly progeny, reborn to a new creation, according to the words of the apostle, 'Our fathers were all...baptized in the sea' (Exod. 15: 20-21). That Mary might always lead the way in man's salvation in her own right, she preceded that people with a canticle, that same people whom the generating waters had put forth.... The name Mary is in the realm of prophecy, salutary to those who are regenerated, the hallmark of virginity, the adornment of modesty, the sign of chastity, a sacrifice to God, the virtue of hospitality, fellowship in holiness.... We have explained why the Mother is a bride, why Joseph is a spouse, why Mary has the maternal name, to show that everything about the birth of Christ has a mystical significance.

MARY: THE NEW EVE

#56 ...*just as a woman had a share in bringing about death, so also a woman should contribute to life. The Mother of Jesus who gave to the world the Life that renews all things was enriched by God with gifts appropriate to such a role.*

Firmicus Maternus, the last early Christian Latin apologist, in his *The Error of the Pagan Religions*, puts Mary in true biblical and historical perspective:

---

[15] Text: CCL 24B.905

c.25[16] God promised Abraham a rule more resplendent than the stars of the heavens. Therefore Mary, the virgin of God, a descendent of the family of Abraham, conceived, that the posterity of the aforesaid men (Abel, Henoch, Noe, Sem, Abraham, Isaac and Jacob) might be united in the bond of an immortal society, and that so the human race, linked in an equal pact of union through a man who was likewise God, should by the merit of obedience attain to the realm of immortality.

The Fathers frequently contrast the disobedience of Eve and the obedience of Mary. Irenaeus is typical in his *Against Heresies*:

3.22[17] In God's design Mary, the virgin, is found obedient (cf.Lc.1:38), but Eve was disobedient, for she did not obey when she was still a virgin...Eve by being disobedient became the cause of death; Mary, although a virgin, by being obedient became the cause of salvation both for herself and for the whole human race.

Pope Innocent III, in a homily *On the Assumption*[18], puts it even more concisely:

For it was fitting that just as by a woman death entered into the world, so by a woman life might return to the world. And so, what Eve lost, Mary saved, so that the source of death might also become the source of life.

Tertullian has an extended treatment of the Eve/Mary parallel in his *On the Flesh of Christ* where he contrasts what happened in Eden with what occurred at the Annunciation:

17.5[19] While still a virgin Eve had allowed to penetrate within her the word that works unto death. Hence it was

[16]Text: CSEL 2.118; cf. ACW 37.101, tr. C.A.Forbes
[17]Text: SC 34.378   [18]Text: PL 217.581   [19]Text: CCL 2.905

necessary that there penetrate within a virgin the word that works unto life, so that the sex which brought about ruin would also be the author of salvation. Eve had believed the serpent; Mary believed Gabriel. The wrong that Eve committed with her believing, Mary, by her believing, rectified.

But, you will say, Eve conceived nothing of the serpent in her womb! 6.Yes, she did. For since from that time onward she brought forth her children in abjection and sorrow, the word of the devil was the seed sown in her, and in due course she brought forth into the world a devil, one who was the murderer of his brother. Mary, on the other hand, gave to the world Him who was, in His time, to be the Saviour of Israel, His brother according to the flesh and the author of his death. Hence God, into Mary's womb, brought about the descent of His Word, the good brother, to destroy the memory of the wicked brother. Christ was to go forth to save man from the very place where man, already condemned, had entered.

Tertullian, in the beginning of his work, *The Dress of Women*, asserts that women, far from dressing ostentatiously, should still be in mourning clothes mourning the sin of the first of the female sex. It betrays a distressing gender gap:

> 1[20] I think you should be dressed in mourning garb, neglecting your appearance, filling the role of mourning and repentant Eve in order to expiate more fully by all forms of penitential dress what women derive from Eve — I mean the ignominy of original sin and the odium of being the cause of the fall of the human race. 'In sorrow and anxiety you will bring forth, o woman, and you are subject to your husband and he is your master' (Gen.3:16). Do you not believe that you are, each one of you, Eve?
>
> The sentence of God on this sex of yours lives on even

[20]CCL 1.343

to this day and so it is necessary that the guilt should also live on. You are the one who opened the door to the devil, you are the one who first plucked the fruit of the forbidden tree, you are the first who deserted the divine law, you are the one who persuaded man whom the devil was not strong enough to attack. All too easily you destroyed the image of God, man. Because of your desert, namely death, even the Son of God had to die.

Justin Martyr, in his *Dialog with Trypho*, is an early witness to the Eve/Mary parallel:

100[21] He became man by the Virgin in order that the disobedience which proceeded from the serpent might receive its destruction in the same manner in which it derived its origin. For Eve, who was a virgin and undefiled, having conceived the word of the serpent, brought forth disobedience and death. But the Virgin Mary received faith and joy, when the angel Gabriel announced the glad tidings to her that the Spirit of the Lord would come upon her, and the power of the most high would overshadow her, wherefore the Holy born of her is the Son of God (Lk.1:35), and she replied, 'Be it done unto me according to your word' (Lk.1:38). And by her He has been born...by whom God destroys both the serpent and those angels and men who are like him, but works deliverance from death to those who repent of their wickedness and believe in Him.

Melito of Sardis, in *On the Pasch*, says:

71[22] He is the lamb being slain,
He is the lamb without voice;
He is the one born from Mary, the lovely ewe-lamb,
He is the One taken from the flock.

And Cyril of Jerusalem in *Catechesis* 12:[23]

[21]Text: PG 6.709   [22]Text: OECT, tr. Hall.   [23]Text: PG 33.741

> Through Eve, while still a virgin, came death; there was
> need that through a virgin, or rather from a virgin, that
> life should appear, that, as the serpent deceived the one,
> so Gabriel should bring the good news to the other.

Jerome, in epistle 22, speaks of 'Eve who as a type of the
Church was created from the rib of her husband' and Zeno
of Verona exclaims: Love, you have restored Eve in Mary,
you have renewed Adam in Christ' (PL 11. 278).

Ephraem, in *Hymn 18 on Blessed Mary*[24] exclaims:

> 24 In Eden Eve became a debtor and the debt by which
> her posterity in their generation were doomed to death
> was written in capital letters. The Serpent, that wicked
> scribe, wrote it out, signed and sealed it with the seal of
> his deceit. Eve was a debtor to sin. But for Mary the debt
> was reserved so that the daughter might pay her mother's
> debt and tear up the handwriting that had handed on her
> mother's tears as a legacy to future generations. ... Since
> Mary was the Virgin inviolate — prefigured by the
> blessed land of Eden before it was furrowed and racked
> — there blossomed from her bosom the Tree of Life...

Zeno of Verona has the fullest statement[25] of the Eve/Mary
parallel in the early Western Church:

> We have spoken of the first circumcision, which is of the
> Jews. Now let us briefly deal with the second spiritual
> circumcision, which belongs to us, which has such power
> that it takes its beginnings from a woman which was
> impossible in the first instance. In a word, the cure of
> circumcision takes its beginnings from a woman, since
> woman was the first to sin. And because the devil by
> insinuating himself persuasively into the ear of Eve had
> wounded and slain her, so Christ entered through Mary's
> ear, dried up all the vices of the heart, and when he was

---

[24]Text: see Palmer, *op. cit.*   [25]Text: CCL 22.28

born of a virgin He cured the wound of a woman. Receive the sign of salvation!

Virginity followed birth as integrity followed corruption. Adam was likewise circumcised by the Lord's cross; because both sexes had received death through a woman who had been the first to lay her hand on the tree, by way of contrast through a man suspended on a tree the whole human race was restored to life. And lest it seem that the point of departure had not been established completely anew, man is first rendered lifeless on the cross, and when He is happily asleep likewise from his side, by the stroke of a lance, without a rib being broken, by water and blood, that is by baptism and martyrdom, a spiritual body of a spiritual female is emitted so that Adam might be legitimately renewed by Christ, and Eve by the Church.

The Immaculate Conception

It is no wonder then that it was customary for the Fathers to refer to the Mother of God as all holy and free from every stain of sin, as though fashioned by the Holy Spirit and formed as a new creature.

The testimony of Augustine to Mary's total freedom from sin comes from his *On Nature and Grace* and is justly famous:

> 36(42)[26] Now with the exception of the holy Virgin Mary in regard to whom, out of respect for the Lord, I do not propose to have a single question raised on the subject of sin — after all how do we know what greater degree of grace for a complete victory over sin was conferred on her who merited to conceive and bring forth Him who all admit was without sin — to repeat then: with the exception of this Virgin, if we could bring together into one place all those holy men and women, while they lived here, and ask them whether they were without sin, what

[26] Text: CSEL 60.263

> do we suppose they would reply?... No matter how they excelled in holiness they would have exclaimed unanimously: 'If we say that we have no sin, we deceive ourselves and the truth is not in us.'

...fashioned by the Holy Spirit into a kind of new substance and new creature...

Anastasius of Antioch, in a *Sermon on the Annunciation*,[27] exclaims:

> Away with death in your case, God-bearer, because you have brought life to men. Away with burial for you, seeing that you have become the divine foundation of inexplicable sublimity. Away with return to dust for you since you are a new formation...

Behold, the Handmaid of the Lord

#57 *The union of the Mother with the Son in the work of salvation is made manifest from the time of Christ's virginal conception up to his death...*

Cyril of Jerusalem, in his *Catechetical Lectures*, instructed the catechumens on how to meet the objections of Jews and pagans to the Virgin birth of Christ:

> 12.28[28] O you Jews, which is more difficult, for a virgin to bear a child, or for a rod to be quickened into a living thing? You admit that at the time of Moses a perfectly straight rod took the form of a serpent and became an object of terror to him who cast it down, and he who before had held fast to the rod now fled from it like a dragon...
>
> 29 These stories, while highly suggestive, are rejected by the Jews who are unimpressed by the argument drawn from the rod so long as there is no reference to births similar to our case, births which are strange and beyond nature.

[27] Text: PG 89. 1377   [28] Text: PG 33.760

Ask them, therefore, the following questions: From whom was Eve begotten at the beginning? What mother conceived her who was without mother? Do not the Scriptures say that she was formed from the side of a man? Why cannot a child be born without a father from the womb of a virgin? Woman owed a debt of gratitude to man, since Eve sprang from Adam, conceived by no mother, but brought forth, as it were, by man alone. Now Mary repaid this debt of gratitude when, through the power of God, of herself alone and not by man, she immaculately brought forth by the Holy Spirit.

Jerome, in his *Against Helvidius*, defends not only the perpetual virginity of Mary but also of Joseph, ruling out the possibility that the Scriptural brethren of the Lord were real brothers and sisters of Christ:

18.16[29] There are things, Helvidius, which, in your abysmal ignorance, you have never read, and you therefore neglected the whole range of Scripture, and employed your madness in outraging the Virgin, like the man in the story who was completely unknown, and finding that he could devise no good action by which he would become well known, burned the temple of Diana, but when nobody revealed his sacrilegious act, it is said that he went up and down himself proclaiming that he was the man who had set the fire. The government of Ephesus were curious to know what drove him to do this, at which he explained that if he could not become well known by good deeds, all men should give him credit for wicked deeds. The history of Greece records this.

But you do worse. You have set fire to the Lord's body, you have defiled the sanctuary of the Holy Spirit from which you are determined to make a team of four brethren and a heap of sisters come forth. In a word, joining in the chorus of the Jews you say: Is not this the carpenter's son? Is not his mother called Mary, and his

[29] Text: PL 23.209

brothers James and Joseph and Simon and Jude? His sisters, too, are they not all with us? (Mt. 13:55).

That the birth of Christ did not diminish His mother's virginal integrity but sanctified it is made clear by Leo the Great in his Epistle to Flavian, called the Tome of Leo:

> 28[30] At the same time the only begotten of the Father eternal was born eternal of the Holy Spirit and the Virgin Mary. And this nativity which took place in time took nothing from, and added nothing to, that divine and eternal birth, but expended itself wholly on the restoration of man who had been deceived ...But that birth so uniquely wondrous and so wondrously unique, is not to be understood in such kind that the properties of His kind were removed through the novelty of His creation. For though the Holy Spirit imparted fertility to the Virgin, yet a real body was received from her body, and, Wisdom building her a house (Prov.9:1), the Word became flesh and dwelt in us (Jn.1:14).

St. Augustine gives unequivocal testimony to Mary's virginity after the birth of Christ:

> s.191[31] The Word of the Father, by whom all time was created, was made flesh and was born in time for us. He, without whose permission no day completes its course, wished to have one day assigned for His human birth. In the bosom of the Father, He existed before all the cycles of ages; born of an earthly mother, He entered upon the course of the years on this day (i.e. Christmas Day). The Maker of man became Man that He, ruler of the stars, might be nourished at the breast; that He, the Bread, might be hungry; that He, the Fountain, might thirst; that He, the Light, might sleep...that He, the Foundation, might be suspended upon a cross....
>
> To endure these, and similar, indignities for us, to free

---

[30] Text: PL 54.758   [31] Text: PL 38.1010

us, unworthy creatures, He Who existed as the Son of
God before all ages, without a beginning, deigned to
become the Son of Man in these latter years...Begotten by
the Father, He was not made by the Father; He was made
Man in the Mother whom He Himself had made, so that
He might exist here for a while, sprung from her who
could never and nowhere have existed except through
His power.

Thus the prediction of the Psalmist was fulfilled:
'Truth is sprung out of the earth' (Ps.84:12) Mary, a
virgin before conception, remained a virgin after child-
birth. Far be it that in this earth, that is, in the flesh out of
which Truth has sprung, integrity should be marred.
Indeed after His Resurrection, when He was thought to
be merely a spirit and not actually corporeal, He said,
Feel me and see; for a spirit does not have flesh and bones
as you see I have (Lk.24:39). Why, then, could He, who as
a grown man was able to enter through closed doors
(Jn.20:19), not pass through incorrupt members as an
infant? To neither the one nor the other of these marvels
do unbelievers wish to give their assent. Therefore, faith
rather believes both, because infidelity believes neither.
In truth, this is that type of unbelief which sees no divinity
in Christ. Furthermore, if faith believes that God was
born in the flesh, it does not doubt that the two miracles
are possible to God, namely that though the doors of the
house were closed, He manifested His mature body to
those within the house, and that as an infant He came
forth, a spouse from His bride-chamber, that is, from the
virginal womb, leaving His mother's integrity inviolate.

The *Diary of Egeria* mentions a Feast of the Presentation in
the Temple:

> 26 [32] The fortieth day after Epiphany is indeed celebrated
> here with the utmost solemnity. There is a procession on
> that day to the Anastasis, and all assemble there for the

[32] Text: CSEL 39.17

liturgy. Everything is performed as prescribed with the greatest solemnity just as on Easter Sunday. All the priests give sermons and the bishop also; and all preach on the Gospel text describing how on the fortieth day Joseph and Mary took the Lord to the Temple, and how Symeon and Anna the prophetess, daughter of Phanuel, saw him, and the words they spoke on seeing the Lord, and of the offering which his parents brought. Afterwards, when all ceremonies have been performed as prescribed, the Eucharist is celebrated and the congregation dismissed.

MARY AND THE PUBLIC LIFE OF JESUS

#58 *In the public life of Jesus Mary appears prominently (from) the Marriage Feast at Cana* [until]. . .*finally she was given by Christ Jesus dying on the Cross as a mother to his disciple: 'Woman, behold thy son' (Jn. 19:26-27).*

The Wedding Feast of Cana has been described as the canonization of neighborliness, so on the face of it it would seem the wrong place for Jesus to choose to rebuke His mother. Yet Christ's cryptic remark to her when she reminded Him that they had no wine (cf. Jn. 2:4) has often been raised as a proof of His insensitivity, if not of obliviousness of her maternity. St. Augustine has some extenuating considerations in his *Tractates on the Gospel of John*:

> VIII.5[33] Unquestionably, there is a mystery here and because of this He appears not to acknowledge His Mother, from whom as the Bridegroom He hath come forth, when He says to her, "Woman, what is it to me and to you? My hour is not yet come" (Jn.2:4). What does this mean? Did He come to the marriage in order to teach men to treat their mothers with contempt? Why, the marriage He was attending was of a man taking a wife with a view

[33] Text: CCL 36.84

to having children. And surely he would wish to be
honored by the children he intended to father. Are we
then to suppose that Jesus had come to the marriage in
order to dishonor His mother on an occasion when mar-
riages are celebrated and wives are married with a view to
having children commanded by God to honor their parents? Unquestionably, brethren, there is some mystery
here.

Now this is a matter of such importance that some have
actually fallen into the very error against which the Apostle has forewarned us: "I fear lest, just as the serpent
seduced Eve by his subtlety so your minds should be
corrupted and fall from the simplicity that is in Christ"(2
Cor. 11:3). Such men set the gospel at naught and assert
that Jesus was not born of the Virgin Mary. And to
bolster their error they would use this passage to support
their view, saying, 'How could she be His mother to
whom He said, "Woman, what is that to me and to you?"'

Jerome angrily rejects the misrepresentation of the text:
Is not his mother called Mary, and his brothers James and
Joseph and Simon and Jude? (Mt. 13:55). Helvidius had the
temerity to misconstrue, 'and his sisters, are they not all with
us?' and to invoke Fathers as proof:

> 18[34] The word 'all' would not be used, you say, if there
> were not a crowd of them. Who, pray, before you came
> on the scene, was acquainted with this blasphemy? Who
> thought the theory worth two cents?...
>
> Feeling himself to be a smatterer, he, Helvidius brings
> forward Tertullian as a witness and quotes the words of
> Victorinus, bishop of Petavium. Of Tertullian I merely
> say that he did not belong to the Church. But as regards
> Victorinus, I assert what has already been proved from
> the Gospel — that he spoke of the 'brothers' of the Lord,
> not at being sons of Mary, but brothers in the sense which
> I have explained, that is to say, in point of kinship, but

[34] Text: PL 23.183

not by nature. We are, however, wasting our time on trifles, and, leaving the fountain of truth, are following diminutive streams of opinion. Could not I line up against you the whole series of ancient writers, Ignatius, Polycarp, Irenaeus, Justin Martyr, and a great many other apostolic, eloquent men, who, against Ebion, Theodotus of Byzantium, and Valentinus, held these same views, and wrote volumes filled with wisdom. Had you ever read what they wrote you would be a wiser man.... You say that Mary did not continue a virgin: I claim even more, that Joseph himself, on account of Mary, was also a virgin so that from a virgin marriage a virgin son was born.

Mary at the foot of the Cross

St. Ambrose, in his *Commentary on Luke*[35] says:

> 7.5 You will be a son of Thunder (like John; cf. Mk.3:17; Jn.19:26) if you are a son of the Church. Let Christ address you also from the Cross: 'Behold your mother'. Let Him say also to the Church: 'Behold your son': then you will begin to be a son of the Church when you see Christ the victor on the cross.

And Origen, in his *Commentary on John's Gospel*, says:[36]

> 1.6 None is Mary's son but Jesus alone; according to orthodox belief about her; when, therefore, Jesus says to His mother, 'Behold thy son, and not 'Behold, this too is thy son' it is as if He said, 'Behold this man is Jesus Himself, to whom you gave birth.' For everyone who has received the fullness that is baptism, lives now no more himself, but Christ lives in him. And since Christ lives in him, the word to Mary applies to him, 'Behold thy son, the anointed, the Christ'.

[35] Text: CSEL 32.84   [36] Text: PG 14:32

MARY AND PENTECOST: MARY ASSUMED INTO HEAVEN

#59 ... *we see the apostles before the day of Pentecost 'persevering with one mind in prayer with the women and Mary the Mother of Jesus' ... (Acts 1:14) Finally the Immaculate Virgin preserved free from all stain of original sin, was taken up body and soul into heavenly glory...*

Cyprian, in his *On the Unity of the Catholic Church* sees a need in his own tepid age to return to the perseverance in prayer that characterized the apostles and Mary in their tight-knit community after the Resurrection:

> 25[37] The common mind prevailed once in the time of the Apostles; this was the spirit in which the new community of the believers, in obedience to the Lord's commands, maintained charity with one another. The Scriptures testify to this: But the crowd of those who had come to believe acted with one mind in prayer with the women and Mary who had been the mother of Jesus, and with his brethren (cf. Acts 1:14). And that was why their prayers were efficacious, that was why they could be confident of obtaining all their requests from God's mercy.
> 26 Among us, however, that unanimity has weakened just as our charitable generosity has disintegrated. In those days they used to sell their houses and estates and store up for themselves treasure in heaven by giving the proceeds to the Apostles for distribution to the poor. But nowadays we do not even give tithes of our possessions and whereas the Lord bids us to sell we instead buy and accumulate.

St. John of Damascus is one of the clearest Patristic witnesses to the doctrine of the Assumption. The following excerpt is taken from his *On the Falling Asleep of the Mother of God*, 2[38]:

---

[37]Text: OECT, ed., Bévenot, 96   [38]Text: PG 96.740

There was need that the body of her who in childbirth had preserved her virginity intact be preserved without corruption after death. There was need that she who carried her Creator as a baby in her bosom, should linger lovingly in the dwelling of her God. There was need that the bride whom the Father had betrothed to Himself should live in the bridal chamber of Heaven, that she who had looked so closely on her very own Son on the Cross, and who experienced there the sword-pangs of sorrow in her heart which she had been spared in child-birth, should look upon Him seated with His Father. There was need that God's Mother should enter into Her Son's possessions, and as Mother of God and handmaid be reverenced by all of creation.

Already in the 4th century the essence of this belief is contained in a homily of Ephrem the Syrian deacon who introduces Mary speaking.[39]

The child whom I bore took me by His eagle's wings and carried me through the sky; and a voice said to me: The heights and the depths which you view shall all belong to your child.

In another homily Ephrem identifies Mary and the Church, pointing out by quoting her the close interconnections between Christ's generation and Christian regeneration as a result of the Redemption and Resurrection:

Mary is saying to Jesus: 'Shall I call thee my son? Or my brother, my spouse, or my Lord? For thou hast given birth to thy mother and rebirth through water. But truly I am thy sister: from the seed of David like thee. And truly I am thy mother, for I conceived thee in my womb. I am thy bride, for thou hast paid the ransom with thy death; thy daughter in rebirth through thy baptism. The Son of the Most High came and rested within me, and I became His mother. Born of me, He in turn has given me rebirth, for He has clothed His mother with a new garment. He has

---

[39]CSCO 186 (Syr. 82), 87, 85, NPNF Ser 2, 13.245

absorbed His own flesh into Himself, and her He has clothed with the sunshine of Himself.'

From at latest the 7th century almost the entire Church, East and West, celebrated the feast of the Assumption. At Rome Pope Sergius (687-707) ordered a procession on that day, as noted in the *Liber Pontificalis*: "He decided that on the days of the Lord's Annunciation, Nativity, and the Dormition of the Holy Mother of God, ever Virgin Mary ...a litany should issue from Saint Hadrian and the people should assemble at Sancta Maria (PL 128.898).

Mary's assumption into Heaven is a logical consequence of her Immaculate Conception. One of the most celebrated, albeit not well preserved, texts on Mary's Immaculate Conception is from Theodotus of Ancyra's *Homily 6* on *Holy Mary, Mother of God*:[40]

> In place of the virgin Eve, mediatrix of death, a virgin has been filled with God's grace to be the minister of life; a virgin has been fashioned possessing the nature of a woman, but without part in her malice; a virgin, inno-cent, without blemish, all-immaculate, inviolate, spot-less, holy in soul and body, who has blossomed as a lily from among thorns, unlearned in the evil ways of Eve. . . When yet unborn she was consecrated to God, and when born was offered to God as a sign of gratitude... Clothed in divine grace as in a garment, her soul filled with a wisdom divine, in heart wedded to God, she received God in her womb, she who is in fact the Mother of God.

We know that a feast of the Assumption was observed in Gaul, preceded by a vigil. Gregory of Tours, in his *Glory of the Blessed Martyrs*, speaks of the miracles in the basilica of the Blessed Virgin Mary, built by the emperor Constantine:

> c.9[41] Mary, the glorious Mother of God, believed to be a virgin after giving birth as before, to the accompaniment

[40]Text: PG 77.1427 cf. DTC 7.906, M. Jugie, 'Immacule Conception'.
[41]Text: PL 71.713

of the angelic choirs, was translated into Paradise, following the Lord.... Her feast is celebrated on January 11; I go to the basilica for the vigil...

III. The Blessed Virgin and the Church

#60 *Mary's function as mother of men in no way obscures or diminishes the unique mediation of Christ, but rather shows its power.*

There are potential possibilities of theological conflict between the concepts of Mary as mediatrix and Christ as sole mediator. Of the latter there can be no doubt.

MOTHER IN THE ORDER OF GRACE

#61 *...in a wholly singular way she cooperated by her obedience, faith, hope and burning charity in the work of the Saviour in restoring supernatural life to souls. For this reason she is a mother to us in the order of grace.*

Mary's maternity in the order of grace began with her act of consent at the Annunciation. In *Hymn 3 on the Annunciation*[42] Ephraem says:

> The Tree of Life, guarded by the Cherub with flaming sword, now has its place in Virgin most pure, guarded by Joseph. The Jews reproach and persecute the Maiden, supposing as they do that Joseph is the father of this Tree. The guard has laid down his sword because the Fruit which he guarded has been sent from on high to earth for the fallen. Mortals ate of it, thereby acquiring life. Blessed is the Fruit that Mary brought forth.

#62 *By her maternal charity, she cares for the brethren of her Son, who still journey on earth.... Therefore the Blessed Virgin is invoked in the Church under the titles of Advocate,*

42Sancti Ephraem Syri Hymmi et Sermones, ed. T. J. Lamy, t3, Cols. 987,989

Helper, Benefactress, and Mediatrix.

Cyril of Alexandria goes into some detail reciting a litany of Mary's activities as mediatrix, in a homily delivered in a church dedicated to her:

> h.4[43] Hail, then, from us, O holy, mystical Trinity, who has assembled us all in this church of Mary, the mother of God! Hail from us, Mary, mother of God, splendid treasure of the whole world, lamp unquenchable, crown of virginity, sceptre of orthodoxy, indestructible temple, dwelling of the uncontainable, mother and virgin, through whom He is called in the holy gospels, 'Blessed is He who comes in the name of the Lord'.
> Hail, thou who contained Him who cannot be contained in your holy, virginal womb, you, through whom the Holy Trinity is glorified, through whom heaven rejoices, through whom angels and archangels are glad, through whom devils are put to flight, through whom the devil, the tempter, fell from heaven, through whom the fallen creature is taken up into heaven, through whom all creation, held prisoner by the madness of idolatry has come to the knowledge of the truth, through whom holy baptism has come to believers, together with the oil of gladness, through whom churches are erected throughout the world, through whom nations are brought to repentance. What more shall I say? Through whom the only-begotten Son of God has shone forth, a light to those who sat in darkness and in the shadow of death (Lk. 1:79), through whom the apostles preached salvation to the nations, through whom the dead are raised, and kings reign.

MARY, A TYPE OF THE CHURCH

#63 *As St. Ambrose taught, the mother of God is a type of the Church in the order of faith, charity and perfect union with Christ.*

[43]Text: PG 77.992

St. Ambrose, in his *On Virginity*, 1.6,31[44]:

> Where is there a woman like to the Church in the number
> of her children? A virgin in her mysteries, a mother of the
> nations, so fruitful is she that the Scripture says of her:
> 'Many are the children of the desolate, more than of her
> that has a husband' (Isa. 53:1). The Church stands
> untouched by evil, and fruitful by the Spirit.
>
> In her motherhood of all the faithful she fulfills the
> deepest mystery of Mary and the Church. The heavenly
> words spoken to the Virgin Mother of God when God
> had become man within her are spoken for all time to the
> Virgin Mother the Church: 'Blessed art thou among
> women'.

And, from the seventh century, we have the testimony of the
monk, Anastasius of Sinai, in his *Hexaemeron*:[45]

> 12 Once again I cry out these words: 'Blessed art thou
> among women', for thou alone, O holy Church, art so
> blessed: thou with thy bridal garland, thou with the bless-
> ing of children, thou, O shining bright Church of God
> and of Christ. Thou alone art blessed among women,
> thou and no other.

Augustine says in one of his sermons:

> s.191,2-3[46] The only-begotten Son of God deigned to
> take upon Himself a human nature taken from a virgin so
> that He might thus link a spotless Church to Himself, its
> spotless founder. In so doing He not only thought of
> virgins undefiled in body, but He also desired that in that
> Church which the apostle, Paul, calls a virgin the minds
> of all should be undefiled. . . . The Church, imitating the
> Mother of God in mind though not in body, is both
> mother and virgin.

[44] Text: PL 16 197   [45] Text: PG 89.1072   [46] Text: PL 38.1010

Augustine tells us that Adam slept while Eve was fashioned from his side; Adam was a figure of Christ, Eve a figure of the Church (PL 36.461). Earlier Tertullian had said: Eve believed the serpent, Mary, Gabriel. What Eve lost by believing, Mary wiped out by her belief (PL 2.782). In Justin's *Dialog* Eve, still an intact virgin, by accepting the serpent's word begot disobedience and death but Mary received the message of the Annunciation with faith and joy:

> 100[47] But the Virgin Mary, filled with faith and joy, when the angel Gabriel announced to her the good tidings that the Spirit of the Lord would come upon her, and the power of the most high would overshadow her, and therefore the Holy One born of her would be the Son of God, answered, 'Be it done unto me according to Thy word.' And indeed she gave birth to Him concerning whom we have shown so many passages of Scripture were written, and by whom God destroys both the serpent and those angels and men who have come to resemble the serpent, but frees from death those who repent of their sins and believe in Christ.

MARY AND CHURCH AS MOTHER

#64 *The Church, contemplating Mary's hidden sanctity, imitating her charity, and faithfully fulfilling the Father's will, by receiving the word of God in faith becomes herself a mother.*

Clement of Alexandria, commenting on the text: 'Blessed is the womb that bore you and the breasts you sucked' (Lk. 11:27), says in the *Paidagogos*:[48]

> 1.6.41 Though women continue to give a flow of milk after they have conceived and given birth, it was not the breasts of women that were blessed by Christ the Lord, the fruit of the Virgin, or named as the true nourishment.

[47]Text: PG 6.712   [48]Text: SC 70.186

No, because now that the loving and kind Father has rained down the Word, it is He Himself who has become the spiritual nourishment of the virtuous.

42. O Mystic marvel! The Father of all is one, the Word who belongs to all is one, the Holy Spirit is one and the same for all. And one, too, is the Virgin Mother. I like to call her the Church. She alone, although a mother, had no milk because she alone never became a wife. She is at once virgin and mother: as virgin, undefiled; as mother, full of love. Calling her children around her, she nourishes them with milk that is holy: the Infant Word. That is why she had no milk, because this Son of hers, beautiful and all hers, the Body of Christ, is milk. The New People she fosters on the Word, for He Himself begot them in the throes of His flesh and wrapped them in the swaddling clothes of His precious blood. What holy begetting! What holy swaddling clothes! The Word is everything to His little ones, both father and mother, educator and nurse. 'Eat my flesh', He says, 'and drink my blood'. He is Himself the nourishment that He gives. He delivers up His own flesh and pours out His own blood. There is nothing lacking His children, that they may grow.

MARY, MODEL OF PERFECTION

#65 *Seeking after the glory of Christ, the Church becomes more like her lofty type, and continually progresses in faith, hope and charity, seeking and doing the will of God in all things.*

Ambrose again, in his work *Concerning Virgins*:[49]

bk.11,c.2 Let, then, the life of Mary be, as it were, virginity itself, set forth in a similitude from which, as from a mirror, the appearance of chastity and the form of virtue is reflected. From this you may take your pattern of life

[49]Text: PL 16.208

showing, in replica, the clear rules of virtue: what you have to correct, to do, and to maintain.

The first thing which inflames the ardor of learning is the greatness of the teacher. Who is greater than the mother of God? Who more glorious than she whom Glory itself chose? Who more chaste than she who bore a body without contact with another body? Why should I speak of her other virtues? She was a virgin not only in body but also in mind, who stained its sincere disposition by no guile. She was humble in heart, grave in speech, prudent in mind, seldom spoken, studious in reading, resting her hope not on uncertain riches but on the prayer of the poor, intent on work, modest in discourse, inclined to seek not man but God as the arbiter of her thoughts, injuring no one, having good-will to all. . . .

Such is the image of virginity. For Mary was such that her example alone is an example to all. If, then, the author does not displease us, let us make trial of what she produces, so that whoever desires for herself the reward may imitate the pattern. How many kinds of virtue shine forth in one virgin? The secret of modesty, the banner of faith, the service of devotion, the virgin within the house, the companion for the ministry, the mother at the temple. In the most holy Virgin the Church has already reached that perfection whereby she exists without spot or wrinkle (cf. Eph. 5:27).

IV. The Cult of the Blessed Virgin in the Church

#66 . . .*following the Council of Ephesus, there was a remarkable growth in the cult of the People of God towards Mary, in veneration and love, in invocation and imitation, according to her own prophetic words: 'all generations shall call me blessed.' (Lk.1:48).*

The basis for Mary's cult was already contained in the New Testament in St. Luke's account of the Divine Infancy. This cult reached its full flowering in the East as a direct result of the unsuccessful attempt of Nestorius to lower

Mary's status. The Christian sentiment was widespread that Mary should be exalted above all angels and men, but that her cult should stop short of giving her the honor reserved for God alone. The lines of orthodoxy are clearly drawn by Epiphanius in his *Panarion of Heresies*:

> 79[50] God came down from Heaven; the Word clothed Himself with flesh from a holy Virgin, not assuredly that the Virgin should be adored, nor to make her god, nor that we should offer sacrifice to her name, nor that now, after so many generations, women should once again be ordained as priests...
>
> He gave her no commission to administer baptism, to bless disciples, nor did He command her to rule over the earth. But this only He enjoined, that she should be a work of sanctification, and should merit to be worthy of His Kingdom...
>
> Let Mary be held in honor, but let the Father, the Son and the Holy Spirit be adored. Let no one adore Mary.

Three stages can be discerned in the evolution of the cult of the Blessed Virgin, the first in the 2nd and 3rd centuries, the second in the Golden Age of Mariology, the 4th and 5th centuries, and the third in the centuries from the mid-fifth to the eighth, following the Council of Ephesus. Ignatius of Antioch is the first Father to mention Mary, and he does so in a theological context. In his *Epistle to the Ephesians* he says:

> 18.2[51] The fact is, our God Jesus Christ was conceived by Mary according to God's dispensation *of the seed of David* (Jn. 7:42), it is true, but also of the Holy Spirit. He was born and baptized that by His Passion He might consecrate the water.

Indeed from the most ancient times the Blessed Virgin has been venerated under the title "Theotokos", "God-bearer".

[50]Text: PG 42.751   [51]Text: SC 10.72

The first absolutely certain witness to the use of the term "Theotokos" to describe Mary is found in a quotation from Alexander of Alexandria as preserved in the *Ecclesiastical History* of Theodoret of Cyrus:

> 1.3[52] We believe next in the one only Catholic and Apostolic Church which is indestructible even if the whole world consorted to fight against it, and which continues victorious over all the impious attacks of the impious, relying on the words of the Master: *Be cheerful! I have overcome the world* (Jn. 16:33).
>
> Next, we believe in the teaching of the resurrection from the dead, of which Jesus Christ our Lord became the first fruits; who bore a body that was real and not just apparent, derived from Mary the God-bearer; in the fullness of time sojourned among the human race for the remission of sins; who was crucified and died, yet suffered no lessening of His Godhead on that account. He rose from the dead, was taken up to Heaven, and sat at the right hand of the Majesty on high.

Vincent of Lerins (d. before 450) gives clear testimony to the doctrine that Mary is truly the Mother of God. In his *Commonitories* he insists that it would be an unforgiveable blasphemy to assert that although one admits that Christ is now one, that there was a time when He was two, not one.... We must assert that humanity has been joined to divinity through the unity of person within the Mother in her womb and, even more, in the Virginal Conception itself[53]:

> 15 ...Through this unity of person, I maintain, and by reason of a similar mystery, it is most truly Catholic to believe (and most impious to deny) that the Word of God Himself was born of the Virgin even as the flesh of the Word was born from an Immaculate Mother.
>
> Wherefore may God forbid that anyone should attempt to deprive Holy Mary of her privileges of divine

[52]Text: GCS 44.22   [53]Text: PL 50.658

grace and her special glory. For by a unique favor of our Lord and God, she is confessed to be the most true and most blessed Mother of God (Theotokos) His Son. She is truly the Mother of God, not merely in name, as a certain impious heresy claims, because, as it alleges, she gave birth to a man who later became God, as we call a woman the mother of priests and bishops because she gave birth, not to a priest or bishop, but to a child who later became one. That is not how Holy Mary is called by me the Mother of God, but rather because, as has already been said, in her sacred womb was accomplished the mystery that, by reason of a certain singular and unique Unity of Person, even as the Word is flesh in flesh, so the Man is God in God.

#67 *Following the study of Sacred Scripture, the Fathers, the doctors and liturgy of the Church, and under the guidance of the Church's magisterium, let them (i.e. theologians and preachers) rightly illustrate the duties and privileges of the Blessed Virgin which always refer to Christ...*

In a not so well-known fragment of Clement of Alexandria there is the following image of Jesus and Mary:[54]

Jesus, a radiant, most pure pearl, whom Mary conceived from the divine Light; for just as a pearl, existing in flesh, and a shell, and moisture seems to be a moist, transparent body, full of life and spirit, so also the incarnate Word God is a spiritual Light gleaming through a lucid, liquid body.

V. Mary, Sign of True Hope and Comfort for the Pilgrim People of God

#68 *...in the glory she possesses in body and soul in heaven...until the day of the Lord shall come (cf. 2 Pet. 3:10), a sign of certain hope and comfort to the pilgrim People of God.*

[54]NPNF 2, 578

The Woman Clothed with the Sun (Rev. 12:1) is generally interpreted by the Fathers to refer to the Church. Hippolytus, in his *Against Anti-Christ*, says:[55]

> 61 By the 'woman clothed with the sun' he meant very clearly the Church, endued with the Father's word, whose brightness is above the sun. And by 'the moon under her feet' he referred to her as being like the moon, with heavenly glory. And the words 'upon her head a crown of twelve stars' refer to the twelve apostles by whom the church was founded. And the words 'she being with child cries, travailing in birth and in pain to be delivered' mean that the Church will not cease to bear from her heart the Word that is persecuted by the unbelievers in the world.

Pope Paul VI in 1967 said: 'The great sign which the apostle Saint John contemplated in the heavens, the woman clothed with the sun (Apoc.12:1) has been rightly interpreted in the Sacred Liturgy of the Catholic Church as the blessed Virgin Mary, Mother of all men by the grace of Christ the Redeemer'.

MARY AND ECUMENISM

#69 ...*among the separated brethren, too, there are those who give due honor to the Mother of Our Lord and Saviour, especially among the Easterns...*

The Decree on Ecumenism of Vatican II pays tribute (#15) to Eastern Christians. 'In this liturgical worship the Christians of the East pay high tribute in very beautiful hymns to Mary ever Virgin whom the Ecumenical Synod of Ephesus solemnly proclaimed to be God's holy Mother, so that, in accordance with the holy scriptures Christ may be truly and properly acknowledged as Son of God and Son of man.'

Likewise the Second Council of Nicaea (787 A.D.) included provisions for the cult of the Blessed Virgin: 'We

[55]Text: PG 10, 780

define with all certitude and diligence that, just as the figure of the precious, life-giving cross is to be exposed, so likewise should venerable, holy images in painting and tesselated work and in whatever other suitable materials be exposed in the holy churches of God, and on sacred vessels and vestments, on walls and on doors, images both of our Lord and Saviour Jesus Christ and of Our Lady immaculate, the holy mother of God, of the honorable angels and of all holy, saintly men.'

We may fittingly conclude with an excerpt from the Akàthistos Hymn which may date from at least as early as the 7th century and which has been called 'the most beautiful, the most profound, the most ancient Marian hymn of all Christian literature':

> Hail to you from whom joy will shine out,
> hail to you through whom the curse will go away,
> hail, redemption of fallen Adam,
> hail, deliverance of the tears of Eve,
> hail, height unattainable by human thought,
> hail, depth invisible even to the eyes of angels,
> hail to you, throne of the King,
> hail to you who bear Him, bearer of all,
> hail, star that heralds the sun,
> hail, womb of divine Incarnation,
> hail to you, through whom creation is reborn,
> hail to you, through whom the creation becomes a child.
> Hail, Virgin Mother, Unwedded Bride.

Epilog

Leander of Seville, in a sermon called *On the Triumph of the Church for the Conversion of the Goths*, celebrates the return of Western Arians to the true fold in Seville, Spain, around 589:

> How sweet is love and how delightful is unity you know well through the prophecy of the prophets, through the divine word of the Gospels, through the teachings of the apostles. Therefore, preach only the unity of nations, dream only of the oneness of all peoples, spread abroad only the good seeds of peace and love. Rejoice, therefore, in the Lord that you were not cheated of your desire, for now, after the ice of winter, after the harsh cold, after the austerity of the snow, like the fruit which is the delight of the fields and the joyous flowers of springtime and the branches smiling with the offshoots of leaves, you have suddenly and joyously recovered those whom you embraced for so long with constant mourning and continual prayers.
>
> Therefore, brethren, let us be glad in the Lord with the full joy of our hearts and let us be jubilant in God our Saviour. Henceforth, we may use the fulfillment of the past as proof that the things that are still awaited shall come true. This has already been said by the Lord in the words: "Other sheep I have that are not of this fold. Them

also I must bring, and there shall be one fold and one shepherd" (Jn.10:16). Behold, we see that this has been fulfilled. Therefore, let us not doubt that the whole world can believe in Christ and come to one Church, since again we have learned in the Gospel by His reassurance: "And this gospel of the kingdom," He said, "shall be preached in the whole world, for a witness to all nations; and then," He said, "will come the end." (Mt.24:14).

Suggested Further Readings

General

Yves M.J. Congar, *I Believe in the Holy Spirit*, 3 vols., New York, 1983.

Henri de Lubac, *The Splendour of the Church*, New York, 1956.

Avery Dulles, *Models of the Church: A Critical Assessment of the Church in All Its Aspects.* Dublin, 1976.

Towards Vatican III. The Work that Needs to be Done, ed., David Tracy, with Hans Küng and Johann B. Metz, New York, 1978.

Chapter I

Joseph C. Plumpe, *Mater Ecclesia. An Inquiry into the Concept of The Church as Mother of God in Early Christianity.* Washington, D.C., 1943.

Chapter II

H.W.M.Rikhof, *The Concept of Church. A Methodological Inquiry into the Use of Metaphors in Ecclesiology.* London, 1981.

Y. Congar, "The Church: The People of God." *Concilium*, 1, (1965) 1.17-19.

Chapter III

P. Huising and K. Wolf, ed., "Electing our own Bishops". *Concilium*, 137, 1980, esp. 3-15,33-47.

C. Journet, *The Church of the Word Incarnate.* Vol.1,*The Apostolic Hierarchy.* New York, 1955.

Chapter IV

Yves M.J.Congar, *Lay People in the Church.* Westminster, Md., 1965.

Chapters V and VI

Louis Bouyer, *History of Spirituality, 1. The Spirituality of the New Testament and the Fathers.* Trans. Mary P. Ryan, New York, 1963.

Chapter VII

Peter Brown, *The Cult of the Saints.* Chicago, 1981.

Chapter VIII

Paul F. Palmer, *Mary in the Documents of the Church.* Westminster, Md.

H. Rahner, *Our Lady and the Church.* Trans. S. Bullough, New York, 1961.

H. Küng and J. Moltmann, ed., Mary in the Churches. *Concilium*, 188, October, 1983.

INDEX